W9-BNM-931

 chicago's 50 best places to find peace and quiet

By Karin Horgan Sullivan

universe publishing

First published in the United States of America in 2005
By UNIVERSE PUBLISHING
A Division of Rizzoli International Publications, Inc.
300 Park Avenue South
New York, NY 10010
www.rizzoliusa.com

© Karin Horgan Sullivan 2005
Cover design by Paul Kepple and Jude Buffum @ Headcase Design
www.headcasedesign.com
Cover Illustration by Sujean Rim
Interior design by Headcase Design

All rights reserved. No part of this publication may be reproduced, stored in a
retrieval system, or transmitted in any form or by any means, electronic,
mechanical, photocopying, recording, or otherwise, without prior consent of
the publishers.

2005 2006 2007 2008 / 10 9 8 7 6 5 4 3 2 1

Printed in the United States of America

ISBN: 0-7893-1346-4

Library of Congress Catalog Control Number: 2005014692

Publisher's Note
Neither Universe nor the author has any interest, financial or personal, in the
establishments listed in this book. No fees were paid or services rendered in
exchange for inclusion in these pages. While every effort was made to ensure
accuracy at the time of publication, it is always best to call ahead and confirm
that the information is up-to-date.

For my wonderful parents,
Steve and Peggy Horgan.

❋ ❋ ❋

Special thanks to my father-in-law,
Frank Sullivan, a lifelong Chicagoan
who was an enormous help in
finding peaceful places.

contents

Outdoor Spaces

introduction

I wish I could claim that such a terrific idea for a book was all mine. But actually, the credit goes to Allan Ishac, author of *New York's 50 Best Places to Find Peace and Quiet*. Some years ago, at a time when Allan was feeling overwhelmed by living in New York City and planning to move away, he was hit by an inspiration. Just as he was falling asleep one night, 10 words flashed in his mind: 25 places to find peace and quiet in New York.

This vision led Allan on a quest to find oases of serenity in the city that never sleeps. Indeed, he found a wealth of urban calm, in places all over the city. He wrote descriptions of them, which he self-published in a guidebook. Within weeks, his 1,500 copies were sold out; soon after, publishers came knocking. Ultimately, Allan stayed in New York, and his little book, now in its third edition, has doubled in size to 50 places. I stumbled across Allan's book on the website of Universe Publishing, which is the publisher of one of my previous books. "What a fantastic idea," I thought. "Chicago needs a guide like this."

And here you have it: the result of my own quest to uncover 50 peaceful places in the big, beautiful, gritty city that I've called home for nearly 20 years. Though you will undoubtedly be familiar with a number of the places I've included, I've tried to stay away from extremely obvious ones. For instance, every neighborhood in Chicago has at least a small park and branch library nearby—just one of the things I love about this city—and you likely have sought refuge there already. What I hope this book does is turn you on to places you may not know about, or may never have thought about exploring.

There are many occasions when you might want to find solitude in the city, so I've included a broad range of places. Some are quiet little corners to duck into downtown, when you need a half-hour escape from the office. Others are outdoor nature areas worthy of several hours' exploration on the weekend. Some are places I've been visiting for years. Others are new discoveries, recommended by Chicagoans from all over the city. But they all provide respite, no matter how brief, and space to renew your soul.

Another thing nearly all the places have in common is that they're free or very low cost. After all, the wealthy can always escape to a luxurious spa, private club, or high-end hotel. I was after places anyone could enjoy, including a visitor on a budget, a local student, or a cash-strapped resident.

One of the biggest surprises was how many areas of natural beauty can be found in and around the city. Having the largest parks system of any U.S. city certainly helps, but even beyond the auspices of the Chicago Park District you can find acres and acres of green space to wander. And don't forget about these places when cold weather settles in; many of these spots, such as the Alfred Caldwell Lily Pool, are just as beautiful, and even more peaceful, after a snowfall as they are in high summer.

It's been a delight to find that Chicago really does offer so many opportunities for tranquility. Whether you're looking for a few minutes' peace or an entire day, I hope this little book will help you find the serenity you seek.

how to use this book

This book is small by design, so that you can keep it in your bag or purse, or even tuck it into your hip pocket. Then when you find yourself craving peace and quiet, your reference for where to find it will be right at hand. You can peruse the table of contents to find the respite that's right for the moment, or take a look at the index. It's broadly organized by area of the city, which is helpful if you have limited time and don't want to travel too far, or if you're an out-of-towner and want a general idea of where you're going.

I've included addresses, phone numbers, hours, price information, and websites where applicable. The beauty of many of these public spaces, however, is that they're open 'round the clock, all year long. If you don't see any opening times listed in an entry, assume you can visit whenever you like. Of course, hours and prices are subject to change, so it's always a good idea to check before you go.

Finally, if you want to use public transportation to get to one of these peaceful places, you can go to the Chicago Transit Authority's (CTA) website (www.transitchicago.com), plug in the address of where you are and where you need to go, and find out which bus or train to take. (You can get the same information by calling 1-888-YOUR-CTA.) Even if you're a city resident who uses the CTA all the time, you'd still be wise to check route and schedule information if you're going to a new part of town; at press time, major transit cuts appeared to be imminent, and many bus lines in particular may be eliminated.

indoor places

❊ aion antiquities + teahouse

chicago's 50 best places to find peace and quiet

ADDRESS: 2135 W. Division Street

Chicago, IL 60622

PHONE: 773-489-1534

HOURS: Tuesday through Thursday, 11 a.m. to 7 p.m.;

Friday through Sunday, 11 a.m. to 6 p.m.;

closed Monday

There's something about a teahouse that inherently seems more civilized than a coffeehouse. Perhaps it's the association with Japanese tea ceremonies, or genteel English teas. Or maybe it's that tea doesn't produce the jittery buzz that coffee does. Whatever the reason, pausing for tea can bring calm to a harried day, and Wicker Park's Aion is a relaxing, down-to-earth place to do it.

Named for the Greek god of indefinitely extending time, Aion was opened several years ago by a longtime collector who thought it would be nice to serve tea alongside the antiques he was planning to sell. But it was the tea that took off, not the antiques, and today Aion boasts a menu of more than one hundred loose-leaf teas, from Assam to White and everything in between. The atmosphere is airy and warm, with a glass storefront, exposed-brick walls, oak floors, and all sorts of maps and unusual antique artifacts from around the world. You can still buy antiques here too (or, confided a waitress, the ones the owner isn't too attached to, which seems to be most of them, judging from the small number of objects with price tags).

Aion serves a delicious high tea any time of day—and for less than half the price charged at upscale hotels downtown. For just $10, you'll be presented with a fabulous two-level tray that includes crumpets, scones, jams, real clotted cream, cucumber and cream cheese sandwiches, spicy tuna sandwiches, thumbprint and shortbread cookies, and a pot of tea of your choice. Not in the mood for all that food? A pot of premium tea is $5, while house teas run only $3.50; cups of tea are available for less. Try the much-raved-about rose petal tea.

Aion frequently hosts bridal and baby showers, so if you plan to drop by on a weekend, you'd be wise to call ahead to make sure it's not booked for a party. Or you can always reserve a table in the cozy, dimly lit downstairs seating room, which has just a handful of tables, a loveseat for lounging, and an ancient-looking mosaic made by the owner. January is the slowest time at Aion, making it the perfect place to come in from the cold and while away a few hours with a pot of tea and a good book.

❋ ando gallery
(at the art institute of chicago)

chicago's 50 best places to find peace and quiet

ADDRESS: 111 S. Michigan Avenue

Chicago, IL 60603

PHONE: 312-443-3600

HOURS: Monday, Tuesday, Wednesday, Friday, 10:30
a.m. to 4:30 p.m.; Thursday, 10:30 a.m. to 8 p.m.;
Saturday and Sunday, 10 a.m. to 5 p.m.

ADMISSION: Fees are suggested—you pay what you
wish, but you must pay something. Suggested admission for adults, $12; children, students, and seniors, $7.
Tuesdays are free.

WEBSITE: www.artic.edu

One of the big challenges in writing this book was that people often were loathe to share their favorite quiet places, fear-
ing that discovery would ruin their solitude. Such was the case
with the Ando Gallery, reluctantly recommended by my friend
Elizabeth, who described it as a favorite, little-known refuge
downtown.

Tucked away in the Art Institute at the back of the T. T.
Tsui Galleries of Chinese Art, the Ando Gallery (#109 on the
Art Institute floor map) is indeed a little treasure. Unlike most
of the other galleries, it's sequestered behind heavy glass
doors that bear the words "please enter," presumably
because the space appears to be off-limits to visitors.

What the doors protect is a quiet, dimly lit room. Standing sentry between the entrance and the display cases is a

grove of 16 oak pillars that architect Tadao Ando designed with the intention that visitors would feel the wind passing through the columns. I can't necessarily say I feel the wind here, but walking through the columns does feel a bit like entering a secret forest.

On the other side of the columns are glass cases holding ancient Japanese silk screens covered with lovely ink paintings, with names like *Landscape of the Four Seasons* and *Eight Views of the Xiao and Xiang Rivers.* Two simple wooden benches provide a spot to contemplate the idyllic natural settings that the paintings depict: craggy mountains, stands of trees, flowing rivers.

The darkened space has an immediate impact on visitors, who tend to lower their voices upon entering. Once, as I sat on the benches enjoying the paintings, I heard a woman say to her companion, "It's an interesting effect, almost sacred." My friend Elizabeth would no doubt agree.

✳ chicago cultural center

ADDRESS: Entrances at 77 E. Randolph Street and

78 E. Washington Street

Chicago, IL 60602

PHONE: 312-744-6630

HOURS: Monday through Thursday, 10 a.m. to 7 p.m.;

Friday, 10 a.m. to 6 p.m.; Saturday, 10 a.m. to 5 p.m.;

Sunday, 11 a.m. to 5 p.m.

ADMISSION: Free

WEBSITE: www.egov.cityofchicago.org

The Chicago Cultural Center was one of the very first quiet places I discovered when I moved to Chicago in 1987. At that time, Chicago didn't have a central library, and the Cultural Center housed many of the main library holdings. My boss at the publishing house where I worked would send me there every once in a while on fact-checking missions for various books we were editing. I fell in love with the beauty and grandeur of the space, and it remains one of my favorite buildings in the city. Today the Cultural Center is home to the Chicago Department of Cultural Affairs, and offers hundreds of free programs, art exhibitions, concerts, and other cultural events each year. It's a great place to wander and feed the senses, particularly in the midst of a dull winter.

This glorious place took five years to build, and when you see it, you can well imagine the anticipation and then the awe with which the public greeted it when the building was finally opened in 1897. The architects were heavily influenced by the design of Italian Renaissance palaces, and they believed that grand form and color should belong to everyone—not just the wealthy. As a result, a plethora of exquisite natural materials were used, and throughout the beaux-arts building you'll find rare imported marbles, Bedford bluestone, solid hardwood, burnished brass, and embellishments created from mother-of-pearl, colored glass, and bits of marble.

The best place to find tranquility here is Preston Bradley Hall, located on the third floor on the Washington Street side of the building. The world's largest Tiffany stained glass dome—a breathtakingly beautiful piece of craftsmanship—tops white marble walls inlaid with intricate mosaic designs in shades of blue, green, and gold. Enormous marble archways open onto east and west wings that are just as sumptuously decorated. The hall is used for a wide variety of concerts, from folk music to opera, but during most of the day it is unused and empty; you'll have your pick of seats to contemplate the lavish beauty here. It's also a great spot to read a book on your lunch hour or enjoy a panoramic view of Millennium Park, just across the street.

☀ chicago school of massage therapy student clinic

ADDRESS: 1300 W. Belmont Avenue, lower level

Chicago, IL 60657

PHONE: 773-880-1397

HOURS: Monday through Friday, 9:30 a.m. to 6:30 p.m.;

Saturday, 9:30 a.m. to 6 p.m.; Sunday, 9:30 a.m.

to 5:30 p.m.

COST: $40 for a one-hour massage

WEBSITE: www.csmt.com/student_clinic.htm

The space may have the sterile feel of a doctor's office, but give the student clinic of the Chicago School of Massage Therapy a chance. You may well come out feeling that you've discovered nirvana.

The student clinic is where massage therapists-in-training practice their skills on real-life clients, and you get a great deal on a massage: $40 for a full hour of stroking, kneading, and working out the kinks. This doesn't buy you much in the way of decor: The clinic is definitely a no-frills kind of place. Massages take place on the lower level of the building in a large, dimly lit, teal-carpeted room curtained off into ten private cubicles. The lack of spa-style aesthetics becomes unimportant, however, once you're reclining on the massage table with your eyes shut. You may hear quiet murmurs and gentle pummeling from the adjacent cubicles, but they soon become just white noise as you lose yourself in the airy, ethereal music playing on the stereo system and surrender to the massage experience. I'm told that the students' instructors poke their heads in every so often to observe, but I've never been aware of them. The bottom line is that the massages I've had here are as good as any professional ones I've had—and they're half the cost.

The student clinic does not take special requests; your massage therapist may be male or female, and may be in the second, third, or fourth and final semester of training. But at such a great price—not to mention their Sunday hours—who's complaining?

❊ christian science reading room

ADDRESS: 62 W. Adams Street
Chicago, IL 60603
PHONE: 312-782-8181
HOURS: Monday, Tuesday, Thursday, Friday, 10 a.m. to 6 p.m.; Wednesday, 10 a.m. to 5 p.m.; closed Saturday and Sunday
ADMISSION: Free

The main purpose of a Christian Science reading room is, of course, to provide a quiet place to study Christian Science literature and to experience a spiritual lift. But the staff here doesn't proselytize, and I've always been left alone to do my own reading. Once during the frenzied holiday season, I even came in to regroup and organize my Christmas shopping list. The space is practically soundproof—though you can see all the cars whizzing by right outside the door on Adams, you can't hear a thing. With the exception of the Chicago Temple (see page 29), I haven't found anywhere else in the Loop that comes this close to being truly silent.

The reading room is a combination bookstore, library, and study area where you'll find books by Christian Science founder Mary Baker Eddy, the Pulitzer Prize–winning *Christian Science Monitor* newspaper, and lots of other Christian and metaphysical writings. You'll also find a very pleasant sitting area that feels like a family living room circa 1970. There are comfy green leather couches that face one another across a large coffee table, and the armchairs scattered about add to the homey feel. The three garish chandeliers provide terrific light for reading. There also is a large conference table with lots of room to spread out, and a computer you can use to go online at no charge for up to half an hour.

Several other Reading Rooms are scattered around the city, at the addresses below. However, the Adams Street location is the only one I've visited, so I can't vouch for the comfort—or the unintrusiveness of the staff—at the others.

North

ADDRESS: 55 E. Wacker Drive
PHONE: 312-236-4671

ADDRESS: 2628 N. Clark Street
PHONE: 773-549-3278

ADDRESS: 2700 N. Pine Grove Avenue
PHONE: 773-549-3362

ADDRESS: 2852 W. Fullerton Avenue
PHONE: 773-227-3062

ADDRESS: 5940 N. Lincoln Avenue
PHONE: 773-728-2596

ADDRESS: 6320 N. Sacramento Avenue
PHONE: 773-764-4159

ADDRESS: 7002 N. Western Avenue
PHONE: 773-764-0278

ADDRESS: 7036 N. Ridge Boulevard

PHONE: 773-764-0300

South

ADDRESS: 4359 S. Michigan Avenue

PHONE: 773-373-4126

ADDRESS: 1933 W. 103rd Street

PHONE: 773-238-3322

❖ division street russian and turkish baths

ADDRESS: 1914 W. Division Street
Chicago, IL 60622
PHONE: 773-384-9671
HOURS: Daily, 8 a.m. to 10 p.m.
ADMISSION: $20

A visit to the Russian and Turkish Baths is an experience straight out of old Chicago. Built in 1906, the baths became a kind of Eastern European fraternity. They were open only to men, and attracted many immigrants who worked long days in sweatshops, then went home to crowded tenements with no indoor plumbing. The baths gave them a place to get cleaned up, and provided them with a place to have a drink and maybe a game of cards with their countrymen. The Division Street baths also became infamous as a place for gangsters and politicians to do business—after all, you can't conceal a wire or a gun when you're wearing nothing but a towel.

The baths have a section for women now, but otherwise, the building and the furnishings retain their old-world character. The facility includes a hot room, heated to 190 degrees Fahrenheit by a giant oven filled with granite stones; the eucalyptus room, where herb-scented billows of steam are guaranteed to clear your sinuses; a Jacuzzi; and a cold pool. Though older Eastern European men are still a common sight, as the neighborhood has changed over the years, the clientele has become more diverse, and now you'll see people of all ages and races relaxing here.

For $20 you get two towels, soap, a locker, and unlimited time to enjoy the baths. You also can opt to pay $25 per half hour for a massage, or $10 for a *placata*, a traditional cleansing treatment in which a masseuse lashes the client with a bundle of oak leaves or seaweed dipped in hot, soapy water. (I'm told it's not painful.) A full restaurant with bar service offers a variety of homemade soups, salads, and entrées. And finally, women can enjoy an extra treat: As of this writing, the owner was planning to offer manicures, pedicures, and facials on the women's side.

❊ 57th street books

ADDRESS: 1301 E. 57th Street

Chicago, IL 60637

PHONE: 773-684-1300

HOURS: Monday through Friday, 10 a.m. to 9 p.m.;

Saturday and Sunday, 10 a.m. to 8 p.m.

WEBSITE: www.semcoop.com

57th Street Books is a real book-lover's bookstore, and a great place to lose track of time. Tucked below street level in Hyde Park, with a wooden sign swinging from a pole out front, 57th Street Books feels like an old-fashioned book shop right out of England.

The space inside is cozy, with low ceilings, exposed-brick walls, and a rabbit's warren of book-lined hallways and rooms. You won't find a café selling lattes or pastries here, just roughly 100,000 titles packed into every conceivable nook and cranny. When you get tired of perusing the shelves, take that stack of books you've undoubtedly accumulated and make yourself at home at the big round library table in the travel section. Or if you want more privacy, you'll find a built-in writing table for one hidden away in room four.

57th Street Books is an expansion of the nearby Seminary Co-op Bookstore, which was founded in 1961 by seventeen people who each chipped in $10 to buy one hundred books and to rent space for the store in the Chicago Theological Seminary. Today more than 40,000 readers have paid $10 to become consumer-owners of the co-op, which also includes the Newberry Library's A. C. McClurg Bookshop. (The Seminary Co-op and Newberry stores focus on academic tomes, while 57th Street carries general-interest titles.) Though you don't have to be a member to shop here, membership does entitle you to a share of the co-op's earnings, plus a 10% discount on most books.

Granted, these financial benefits aren't huge. But independent bookstores are a dying breed in this country, and without customer support, places like 57th Street Books will become relics of the past. Making sure that doesn't happen is worth a lot more than $10.

❊ first united methodist church at the chicago temple

ADDRESS: 77 W. Washington Street

Chicago, IL 60602

PHONE: 312-236-4548

HOURS: Sanctuary open daily from 7 a.m. to 9 p.m.

ADMISSION: Free

WEBSITE: www.chicagotemple.org

I've avoided recommending churches, mainly because they're such obvious places to find peace and quiet, and because it hardly seems fair to pick just a few when there are dozens (if not hundreds) of worthy ones all over the city. But after visiting the First United Church, I felt that its unusual location—right across from Daley Plaza, in one of the busiest, densest parts of the Loop—more than justified its inclusion.

First United is the oldest congregation in Chicago, founded by Methodist circuit riders in 1831. As the membership expanded, it built several successively bigger churches here at the corner of Washington and Clark streets. In the early 1920s, church leaders received a great deal of pressure to sell their increasingly valuable plot of downtown real estate and follow the growing trend to move to the suburbs. According to church officials, though, they were inspired by great Chicago architect Daniel Burnham's exhortation to "make no little plans." Consequently, they not only decided to stay put but also to erect a beautiful church in their existing spot, one that would stand up to the buildings around it. The result is the

Chicago Temple, which at the time was the tallest building in the city. It's a striking example of Gothic architecture with an eight-story spire that remains the world's tallest steeple.

No matter what your religious persuasion, the church sanctuary is a lovely place to find solitude during the day. Richly patterned stained glass windows glow with color on even the dreariest of days, and the wooden pews have been worn to a comfortable smoothness over the decades. The atmosphere is one that encourages quiet contemplation, reflection, and tolerance. Not in a church kind of mood? You also can find respite in the second-floor sitting room, a large lobby that offers several comfortable sofas and armchairs.

❋ garfield park conservatory

ADDRESS: 300 N. Central Park Avenue

Chicago, IL 60624

PHONE: 312-746-5100

HOURS: Friday through Wednesday, 9 a.m. to 5 p.m.;

Thursday, 9 a.m. to 8 p.m.

ADMISSION: Free

WEBSITE: www.garfieldconservatory.org

Those of us on the west side of the city have long known about a horticultural gem that remains largely unnoticed by much of the rest of Chicago: the Garfield Park Conservatory. Though this enormous venue received tens of thousands of visitors in 2002, when it provided the backdrop for a fantastic exhibition that glass artist Dale Chihuly designed specifically for the conservatory, it returned to being quietly magnificent once the hubbub died down. I've included the conservatory in the "Indoor Places" section because its greenery is such a welcome sight in the winter; but its outdoor amenities just as easily qualify it as a wonderful outdoor place too.

When it opened in 1908, the conservatory was considered revolutionary. Back then, conservatories tended to feature plants isolated in pots and stiffly displayed on columns or arranged in the center of a room. But Jens Jensen, who was the superintendent of what at the time was the city's West Park System, had something different in mind. A passionate conservationist who is considered one of the major figures of Prairie School landscape architecture, Jensen created what looked like outdoor landscapes with plants set in the ground around a central fountain or pond. One of the most pleasant spots is the Aroid House, where a secluded wooden bench sits among prehistoric-size greenery bordering a koi pond. A rushing waterfall provides the only sound, and several chartreuse and golden glass lily pads "float" in the pond—permanent installations from the Chihuly exhibition.

I love to visit the conservatory in mid-winter, when my cabin fever is at its height and I feel positively desperate to inhale the warm, woodsy aroma of soil and green living things. The Spring Flower Show, which always opens sometime in February, is a great antidote to the winter doldrums. Azaleas, camellias, daffodils, tulips, and hundreds of flowering annuals in blazing hues fill the senses with color and aroma, giving me the strength to slog through another couple of months until spring arrives.

When warm weather finally comes, the many outdoor pleasures of the conservatory reveal themselves. There's a gravel labyrinth for walking in solitary contemplation. Beyond this, situated on a plot of land the size of a typical city lot, is the Demonstration Garden, which is used to host educational presentations about various aspects of gardening, such as raised-bed planting, beekeeping, composting, and techniques to use and beautify small urban spaces. It's a rustic, appealing spot, with gravel pathways, vine-covered trellises made from twigs, and a wooden pergola hung with painted gourds.

Beyond the Demonstration Garden is the City Garden, a stunning 12-acre space anchored by a dramatic, sloping lawn. The landscapes surrounding the lawn flow gently into one another over sculpted earth mounds. The feel is open and airy as you stroll along winding paths, past the lily pond and waterfall, through the ornamental grove, and up the hill to the perennial garden and 25-foot-high overlook with a magnificent view of the grounds. Green Line trains occasionally rumble by, but aside from these interruptions, you're free to engage in a green reverie for as long as you like.

✳ grainger hall of gems, grainger gallery, hall of jades (at the field museum)

ADDRESS: 1400 S. Lake Shore Drive

Chicago, IL 60605

PHONE: 312-922-9410

HOURS: Daily, 9 a.m. to 5 p.m. (last admission at 4 p.m.)

ADMISSION: Adults, $10; children 3 to 11, $5; seniors
and students, $7. Monday and Tuesday generally are
free in the fall and winter.

WEBSITE: www.fieldmuseum.org

With its palatial, reverberant main lobby frequently mobbed by schoolchildren and tourists, the Field Museum may not strike you as a likely place to find tranquility. But upstairs, tucked away at the southern end, is a little oasis of calm where you'll find several pleasant spots for respite.

In the southwest corner, the Grainger Hall of Gems is a darkened room where more than three hundred precious stones, crystals, and minerals sparkle in glass cases, with the cantaloupe-size Chalmers topaz as the centerpiece. Soothing New Age music floats down from the ceiling, and the only light comes from within the displays. Visiting this little gallery feels like discovering a secret cavern, one that glitters with every color of the rainbow.

There are no benches in this gallery, so when you're tired of standing head to the Grainger Gallery. This long, carpeted hallway is scattered with upholstered benches, and, unlike much of the museum, sound here is absorbed and muffled. Displays of ancient Buddhist and Daoist artifacts enhance the ambiance.

Continue through the gallery and you'll arrive at another wonderful little spot—the renovated Hall of Jades. While it doesn't have the womblike feeling of the Hall of Gems, it has the advantage of several wooden benches that make it more comfortable. There are no videos or interactive displays here, just softly lit jade objects dating as far back as 3300 BCE. It's educational too—I never knew that jade came in so many colors, from pearly gray to luminous bright green and shades of tan and brown. Sit here for as long as you like, until you find the strength to rejoin the crowds on the lower level.

✻ healing earth resources

ADDRESS: 3111 N. Ashland Avenue

Chicago, IL 60657

PHONE: 773-EARTHLY (327-8459)

HOURS: Monday through Saturday, 10 a.m. to 9 p.m.;

Sunday, 10 a.m. to 7 p.m.

WEBSITE: www.healingearthresources.com

Healing Earth Resources isn't just a quiet place to visit; it's also a great source for tools that will help you to nurture inner peace wherever you may be. Husband-and-wife owners Michael Wisniewski and Dawn Silver have created a New Age mecca of sorts, where you can find books and products oriented toward self-help and spirituality, as well as a weekly meditation class; a healing circle, where for a $5 donation participants can receive whatever healing treament is being offered that evening, such as Reiki or chakra balancing; a film viewing and discussion group; a regularly scheduled "Socrates potluck," where people get together to discuss life's big questions over a potluck meal; yoga classes; and more. Sure, a lot of it may be a little touchy-feely for some people, but the intention here is all about fostering goodness in the world—and what could be more peaceful than that?

Painted in bright hues of yellow, lime, and turquoise, the space has a cheerful feeling, with an eclectic mix of prayer flags, candles, and Buddhist art decorating the walls. Soothing music often plays in the background, while incense and aromatherapy products enhance the aural ambiance.

I like the small sitting area, which has a couch and a couple of chairs. On a table there is a prayer book where visitors can write prayers and offer blessings. Some of the writings are emotional, like the pleas for the recovery of a sick loved one or thanks for good fortune. One of my favorite entries is this simple blessing from a teenager:

> "May peace be in Chicago—
> may peace be in the world—
> may peace be with you—
> Always."
>
> —*Ian, age 16*

Spread the word.

✳ lincoln park conservatory

ADDRESS: 2391 N. Stockton Drive

Chicago, IL 60614

PHONE: 312-742-7736

HOURS: Daily, 9 a.m. to 5 p.m.

ADMISSION: Free

In the dead of winter, when all of Chicago is the color of months-old slush, the Orchid Room at the Lincoln Park Conservatory will make you swoon. The perfume of the flowers is positively intoxicating, and their colors are so saturated they practically vibrate. It's the kind of place that wakes you up and makes you glad to be alive.

Each of the rooms at this Victorian-era conservatory has its distinct charm. The Palm Room provides a warm, humid home for plants that trace their roots, so to speak, back to the time of the dinosaurs. The plants here are enormous, making it easy to imagine a time when gigantic creatures roamed the earth. It's humbling, too, to see living things that have withstood change for millions of years—it's a bit of prehistory right in our own backyard.

Descend the staircase to the more secluded Fern Room, where you'll find a pleasant spot with a bench near two trickling waterfalls. For the past several years, the Fern Room has been the backdrop for a series of "sound installations," pieces of music and other sounds composed specifically for the conservatory. One piece, for instance, extracted rhythms and pitches from sounds recorded throughout the city, then blended them into subtle waves of sound that build and recede.

The Show House changes its display to reflect the seasons. My favorite is the Spring Flower Show, which opens in mid-February with an explosion of color just when I crave it most.

Outside in the spring and summer, the Great Garden in front of the conservatory displays annual flowers in a formal garden, while Grandma's Garden across the street is a more informal English garden. The masses do tend to come out when the weather warms up, but if you can drop by the gardens on a weekday in early spring, you'll likely enjoy a blissfully uninterrupted visit.

❖ north pond restaurant

chicago's 50 best places to find peace and quiet

ADDRESS: 2610 N. Cannon Drive

Chicago, IL 60614

PHONE: 773-477-5845

HOURS: Lunch (June through September only), Tuesday
through Saturday, 11:30 a.m. to 2 p.m.; dinner, Tuesday through Sunday, service starts at 5:30 p.m.; Sunday brunch, 11 a.m. to 2 p.m.; closed Monday

WEBSITE: www.northpondrestaurant.com

I debated long and hard about including this spot in the book. I wanted every place to be free or low cost, because peace and quiet should be available to everyone in the city, not just the wealthy. At about $25 for just an entrée, the cost of a meal at North Pond puts it out of reach of many people.

But the setting and cuisine compelled me to add it. One reviewer said that eating at North Pond is like "dining in a nature preserve." It's an entirely apt description, despite the eatery's proximity to one of the busiest sections of the city. The restaurant is situated in the middle of Lincoln Park (the actual park, not the neighborhood), right on the banks of the body of water for which it's named. (Before it was a restaurant, the building was used as a warming hut for skaters.) You can't even drive to the restaurant's entrance, because it's not actu-ally on any street; you have to walk through an underground tunnel at Lakeview and Deming to reach it.

It's worth the small effort—and perhaps a specially accu-mulated dining fund—to eat here, because the food is sublime.

Chef Bruce Sherman, a founding member of the city's Green City Market, changes the menu frequently, indulging his passion for fresh, locally grown, seasonal ingredients. When my husband and I visited North Pond on a cold night in November for his 40th birthday, the autumnal meal we had warmed us to our bones: fennel soup; a salad of heirloom beets and mint; squash gnocchi in brown butter with hazelnuts, apple, and shaved Parmesan; a symphony of autumn vegetables that included a spinach strudel and a fabulous squash tart; and for dessert, a finale of miniature chocolate delights.

The warm arts-and-crafts decor is as wonderful as the food. We were lucky enough to sit by the fireplace, which is surrounded by three walls of nine-foot-tall glass doors that provide a spectacular view of the pond, the park, and the city skyline. (In the summer the doors are thrown open, erasing the boundary between indoors and out.) Nurtured by a meal that echoed the rhythms of nature, we were entirely content, troubled only by the uncertainty of when we might possibly return.

❊ oriental institute museum

chicago's 50 best places to find peace and quiet

ADDRESS: 1155 E. 58th Street

Chicago, IL 60637

PHONE: 773-702-9514

HOURS: Tuesday and Thursday through Saturday,

10 a.m. to 6 p.m.; Wednesday, 10 a.m. to 8:30 p.m.;

Sunday, noon to 6 p.m.; closed Monday

ADMISSION: Free, but suggested donation of $5 for

adults and $2 for children under 12

WEBSITE: www.oi.uchicago.edu

Chicago has scores of world-class museums, but not all of them offer much peace and quiet, thanks to the large crowds that frequently visit. One that never fails to maintain its serenity, however, is the Oriental Institute Museum in Hyde Park. Inside the ivy-covered stone building you'll find a beautiful space painted in soothing tones of paprika and slate blue. Light spills down from fixtures designed to resemble Bronze Age Palestinian pots, and antique-looking motifs from Egypt and Mesopotamia adorn the ceilings. Ancient history resides here, and patrons seem to respond with a quiet reverence.

The museum's Mesopotamian Gallery presents a rare opportunity to see artifacts from the rich culture of ancient Iraq, including pottery, metal pieces used as money, glass vessels, and one of the earliest writing systems. Considering Mesopotamian history dates back roughly six thousand years, it's amazing to contemplate how advanced the culture was, with sophisticated systems of mathematics, astronomy, and transportation. When I'm here I can't help but reflect unfavorably on our disposable society—who's going to be excited about unearthing diapers and plastic razors in a thousand years? Towering over the gallery is the colossal *lamassu*, a huge, 40-ton stone sculpture of a winged bull with a human head. My favorite pieces, though, are the Striding Lions—molded brick panels glazed in beautiful shades of turquoise, white, and ochre that centuries later are still resplendent.

The other galleries at the museum hold artifacts from Egypt and Persia (now Iran). If you're lucky, Margaret will be at the security desk. The ancient Orient is her area of expertise, and in more peaceful times, she conducted research in Iraq. She can answer just about any question you might have about the museum.

✳ ritz-carlton lobby

ADDRESS: 160 E. Pearson Street

Chicago, IL 60611

PHONE: 312-266-1000

ADMISSION: Free

WEBSITE: www.fourseasons.com/chicagorc/#

Technically, hotel lobbies are for the comfort of guests, not the general public. But as long as you behave yourself and don't start unpacking a picnic lunch, no one is likely to hassle you about taking a seat in one. After all, how do they know you're not waiting for a guest or a business appointment?

One of the most comfortable hotel lobbies can be found on the 12th floor of the Ritz-Carlton, behind Water Tower Place. Take the elevator just inside the hotel entrance to the 12th floor; when the elevator doors glide open, you're greeted with a subdued setting of peach-and-green luxury. Anchoring the space is a sun-drenched atrium with a reflecting pool in the center. Potted palms and greenery surround the pool, beyond which are many nooks with comfy armchairs and couches, perfect for relaxing or quiet conversation.

If you're seeking more solitude, walk through the lobby and bear to the left, where you'll find a long, carpeted hallway with several arrangements of couches, chairs, and coffee tables. At the end of the hallway is a rocky pool of water with waterfalls and greenery, and a skylight overhead. It's completely quiet here, except for the sound of water tumbling over the rocks, making this a great place to do some reading or to boot up your laptop and work.

Other hotel lobbies where you'll find anonymity and a cushy seat include **the Drake** (140 E. Walton Place), **the Four Seasons** (120 E. Delaware Place, 12th floor), **the Palmer House** (17 E. Monroe), and **the Park Hyatt** (800 N. Michigan Avenue).

✳ russian tea time

ADDRESS: 77 E. Adams Street

Chicago, IL 60603

PHONE: 312-360-0000

HOURS: Tuesday through Thursday, 11 a.m. to 11 p.m.;
Friday and Saturday, 11 a.m. to midnight; Sunday and
Monday, 11 a.m. to 9 p.m. Afternoon tea: daily, 2:30
to 4:30 p.m.

Pausing for refreshment at Russian Tea Time means enjoying the comforts of another world. Elegant but unpretentious, this delightful establishment features subdued lighting from brass chandeliers, plush burgundy draperies and booths, dark wood trim, and antique samovars. In the background, the sound of softly playing *balalaika* music adds to the cozy, intimate feeling that I imagine to be akin to having tea in a Russian grandmother's living room.

Owned by Uzbek immigrants, the restaurant offers a full menu of Russian, Slavic, and Eastern European comfort foods—and, surprisingly, there's plenty here to please vegetarians too. What I enjoy at Russian Tea Time, though, is afternoon tea, served every day between 2:30 and 4:30. For $19, you can choose a pot from nearly three dozen teas, accompanied by a scone, an assortment of savory mini-sandwiches, and a variety of sweets. If you're not hungry enough for such a large spread, or if you're too late for afternoon tea, I highly recommend a raisin scone, served warm with Devonshire cream, lemon curd, and strawberry marmalade. Tender and light, Russian Tea Time's scones have made me forever disdainful of the rocklike biscuits many coffeehouses try to pass off with the same name.

Because of its proximity to the Art Institute and Orchestra Hall, the restaurant can be busy just before and after a performance, so you may want to steer clear at dinnertime or at least make a reservation.

Looking for a romantic spot to propose? Russian Tea Time claims to have provided the backdrop for numerous engagements with a "100% acceptance rate."

❄ spacetime tanks flotation center

ADDRESS: 2526 N. Lincoln Avenue

Chicago, IL 60614

PHONE: 773-472-2700

HOURS: Monday through Friday, noon to 11 p.m.;

Saturday, 10:30 a.m. to 10:30 p.m.; Sunday, 10:30 a.m.

to 7:30 p.m.

COST: $40 for a one-hour float

WEBSITE: www.spacetimetanks.com

NOTE: Appointments are strongly recommended.

An hour in one of the SpaceTime sensory-deprivation tanks is as close to going back to the womb as you can get in this lifetime. Climb in the tank, close the door, then lie back, shut your eyes, and effortlessly float in water that's been loaded with eight hundred pounds of Epsom salts and heated exactly to skin temperature. What do you hear? Nothing but your own breath and heartbeat. Feel your limbs relax as you become one with the warm, salty water.

Flotation tanks were first created in the 1950s by a scientist at the National Institute of Mental Health, who found that when deprived of all stimuli, people could achieve both extreme relaxation and heightened states of awareness. I can attest that floating at SpaceTime is one of the most profoundly relaxing experiences you're likely to have. Falling asleep during a float is extremely common; there's no danger of drowning, because the water is so dense you can't flip over.

On its website, SpaceTime posts drawings and writings people have done after they float. Entries describe "a mind-expanding, emotion-digging experience" and "the one tunnel that leads to ultimate imagination, relaxation, freedom." Another says, "I was able to just be."

On your first visit, you might find the experience a bit unsettling. All those Epsom salts create a distinctive odor that's a bit unpleasant until you get used to it. Also, it's disconcerting to climb into an eight-foot tank that's so dark you can't see all the way into it, and then shut yourself in. (The doors don't lock.) But give yourself over to the experience, and you'll soon feel all your stress and tension drift away.

❖ thousand waves spa for women

chicago's 50 best places to find peace and quiet

ADDRESS: 1212 W. Belmont Avenue

Chicago, IL 60657

PHONE: 773-549-0700

HOURS: Tuesday through Friday, noon to 9 p.m.; Satur-

day and Sunday, 10 a.m. to 7 p.m.; closed Monday

COST: $20 for three-hour spa-bath visit

WEBSITE: www.thousandwavesspa.com

Thousand Waves is one of my all-time favorite places in the city, not just because it's an oasis of serenity but also because the low admission fee makes it possible to indulge in a spa visit without spending a lot of money. And unlike many spas, where you might feel like you have to be perfectly toned and model-thin just to cross the threshold, Thousand Waves draws an extremely diverse female clientele: straight and gay, young and old, skinny and fat, white and brown, and everyone in-between.

This is one of my favorite places to go during cold weather when I need a break from the rest of the world. For just $20, you get three hours at the spa, which has a dry red-wood sauna, a eucalyptus steam bath, and a Jacuzzi. You don't have to bring anything but yourself, because the spa provides a kimono robe, washcloth, towel, rubber sandals, soap and shampoo, hair dryers, and a locker to use, all at no additional charge. Clothing is optional, and most visitors opt to go *au naturel*. (Frankly, the few women I've seen in bathing suits have been ones with model-lithe bodies; my friends and

I, with our sundry scars of motherhood, feel perfectly comfortable going nude. Go figure.) It also offers other spa services, like massages and herbal wraps, for an additional cost. The price of all services includes an hour of spa bath time.

When you're ready to take a break from steaming and soaking, go downstairs to the relaxation room, a serene, Zen-like space that used to be a karate studio. Help yourself to a complimentary cup of herbal tea, then relax with one of the many magazines available, or curtain yourself off in one of the napping cubicles and take a rest.

Thousand Waves offers a wonderful service that I hope I'll never have to use: the Stress Management Program for Women with Cancer. (Thousand Waves is owned by breast cancer survivor Nancy Lanoue and her life partner Sarah Ludden; Lanoue originally owned the spa with partner Jeanette Pappas, who died of pancreatic cancer in 1989.) To help women cope with cancer, the spa offers *free of charge* five spa visits and five one-hour massages to any woman diagnosed with cancer. I can't think of a better place to feel nurtured if you're ill.

✳ union station great hall waiting room

ADDRESS: 210 S. Canal Street

Chicago, IL 60606

HOURS: Daily, 5 a.m. to 12:30 a.m.

There's a good chance you have been in Union Station dozens, maybe even hundreds, of times without seeing the magnificent Great Hall Waiting Room. Commuter and Amtrak trains chug into and out of the concourse on the east side of Canal Street, and passengers may think they have no reason—or time—to dawdle in the waiting room on the west side. In fact, the first time I visited the Great Hall, I wasn't even sure it was open, there was such a dearth of activity around it.

Finding the doors unlocked, I started down one of several rather gloomy marble staircases. Curiously, the light grew brighter the farther I descended below street level, until finally I found myself in a sun-soaked, awe-inspiring space.

One of the few turn-of-the-century depots left in the country, the Great Hall Waiting Room evokes another era, when trains were the fastest way to travel, and Chicago was the king of railway hubs. Completed in 1925, the colossal beaux-arts building features a 112-foot-high vaulted skylight, pink marble floors, tan marble walls, and gold-topped Corinthian columns. At the south end, rows of long wooden benches have been worn smooth over the decades, as have the marble stairs, where the treads are so uneven in spots that they appear to undulate.

Given the millions of travelers who've passed through these portals, it's hard to believe how hushed the waiting room is (except for rush hour, of course). Whether you see businesspeople, families, or young trekkers with backpacks wandering in from the tunnel that connects the two halves of Union Station, they tend to speak in quiet tones, perhaps in reverence for the magnificence of the space. Whatever the reason, I'm grateful. The benches make a wonderful escape from the office, whether for reading a book, having a bite to eat, or just sitting back and letting your imagination transport you to another, more civilized time.

❄ the winter garden at harold washington library

ADDRESS: 400 S. State Street

Chicago, IL 60605

PHONE: 312-747-4999

HOURS: Monday through Thursday, 9 a.m. to 7 p.m.;

Friday and Saturday, 9 a.m. to 5 p.m.; Sunday, 1 to 5 p.m.

ADMISSION: Free

WEBSITE: www.chipublib.org

I'm always surprised by how few people visit this enormous, light-drenched hall on top of the Harold Washington Library. It's one of the city's great atrium spaces, with a one-hundred-foot-high glass ceiling above an airy, open room designed to resemble the courtyard of a country villa.

Yet the Winter Garden always has an undiscovered feel to it, perhaps because the visitor has to work a bit to find it. You must first make your way up a series of escalators to the third floor, transfer to another set of escalators for the next five floors, then finally take a separate, tucked-away escalator or elevator the rest of the way up. The reward for this effort, though, is a delightfully tranquil space with copious natural light and a great view. The handful of tables scattered around the room provide a place to work, read, or even eat lunch.

The Winter Garden can be a useful escape in cold weather, but I actually find it much more appealing in the summer. The broad, gray marble floors and slate blue walls give it a cool feel. Calling it a "garden," quite frankly, is a bit of a stretch, given that it consists of four olive trees in planters and some ivy half-heartedly creeping up the walls. But the sparseness of the room can be most welcome on a hot day, when you need a breather but can't bear to forsake air-conditioning.

outdoor spaces

❊ the adler planetarium lawn

ADDRESS: 1300 S. Lake Shore Drive

Chicago, IL 60605

PHONE: 312-922-STAR (7827)

ADMISSION: Free

WEBSITE: www.adlerplanetarium.org

NOTE: If you drive, take plenty of quarters; meters oper-
ate 24 hours, and a quarter buys only a half-hour.

I discovered the charm of this spot on the lake after a friend told me that when he and his wife were courting thirty years ago, they used to take a bottle of wine and go to the planetarium at dusk. They'd sit on the lawn for a couple of hours, sharing the wine and watching the lights of the city come on.

This sounded like a perfect (and cheap) date, so one hot evening in July, I got a baby-sitter, packed a picnic, and took my husband to the planetarium, where we discovered this truly is a delightful spot to take in the city at night.

The best time to go is around 7:30 p.m., after the folks with video cameras and young families with gamboling children clear out, and night is just beginning to fall. The sun setting behind the Sears Tower casts a pinkish light on the lake, and the water is mesmerizing as it undulates and shimmers in the bay created by the Museum Campus. The only sounds are the cries of seagulls overhead and the sound of the water lapping at the shore below. With its location at the end of a peninsula that juts out into the lake, Adler is a wonderful place to catch the lake breezes and cool off. Even on a hot day, in fact, you may need a sweater as night falls. The lawn on the north side has the most privacy, and you'll see the skyline from the Shedd Aquarium north to the Hancock Building.

It's remarkable to see so much of the city at once and yet have such a strong sense of distance from it. Without the grating urban sounds, you can revel in this beautiful, serene view of the city. The only inkling of urban life is the traffic on Lake Shore Drive. And at this distance, it sounds more like the white noise of the ocean.

✳ alfred caldwell lily pool

ADDRESS: Fullerton Avenue at Cannon Drive

Chicago, IL 60614

PHONE: 312-747-2474

HOURS: Monday through Friday, 7:30 a.m. to 4:30 p.m.;

Saturday and Sunday, 9 a.m. to 4 p.m.

ADMISSION: Free

Tucked behind the stone Lincoln Park Zoo sign at Fullerton Avenue and Cannon Drive, this lush urban oasis is so well hidden that a friend who lived in the neighborhood for several years had no idea it even existed.

The pond is named for Alfred Caldwell, the architect who designed the one-and-a-half acre space for the Chicago Park District in 1938. Profoundly influenced by the great Prairie School architects Frank Lloyd Wright and Jens Jensen, Caldwell created an homage to the midwestern landscape by using plants indigenous to the Great Plains and limestone slabs that echo the horizontal quality of the terrain here. Caldwell was way ahead of his time in his passion for native prairie plants such as echinacea and blazing star, which today are so popular here. In fact, Caldwell was so committed to his vision that when the park district slashed his budget, he got his wife's consent to cash in his life insurance policy to fund the plantings around the pond.

Caldwell's creation was under-appreciated at the time, however, and almost immediately fell into decline. The Lincoln Park Zoo used it as a rookery—a home for bird colonies—for many years, and the combination of birds, foot traffic, and invasive trees denuded the banks of the once-beautiful pond. Finally, in the 1990s, Friends of Lincoln Park and the Chicago Park District got together and raised money to restore the pond to its former glory.

You can enter the pond from the zoo parking lot, just south of Fullerton on Cannon Drive, but I prefer the more interesting Prairie-style stone-and-wood entrance on Fullerton, just west of Cannon. A few paces inside the Fullerton entrance, you'll come to the waterfall that feeds the pond. Water tumbles over thin planks of limestone, then flows under the walking path and into the pond, where it becomes quiet and placid. Next to the waterfall, large limestone slabs provide ample room to sit in the sun. After you've had your fill of the waterfall, follow the stone path encircling the pond, where grasses and native plants grow completely wild right up to the edges of the path. On a warm summer morning, it feels like walking through a meadow resounding with birdsong.

Stone slabs set amidst the plants provide many places to sit in silence. Near the south end of the pond are two interlocking stone-and-wood pavilions. I like to sit on the little stone steps inside the southernmost pavilion, where the air remains cool even on a hot day. Tucked away here in the shade, I have the sense of being far away; I can see only the tranquil pond and the dragonflies flitting above it. Caldwell believed that being close to nature would have a "civilizing effect" on the masses. I can't speak for the masses, but it certainly has a civilizing effect on me.

❊ aon center courtyard

ADDRESS: 200 E. Randolph Street

Chicago, IL 60601

PHONE: 312-228-8200

ADMISSION: Free

My very first job out of college, in 1987, was at a book publisher on Michigan Avenue. As a brand-new transplant from a Cincinnati suburb, I loved the big city, but at times I found it overwhelming. How I wish I had known then about the pleasant, shady plaza just two blocks away at the high-rise formerly known as the Exxon Building, now called the Aon Center. Unless you regularly walk past the Aon Center, you may well have no idea the plaza is there. Situated a story below street level, it's one of those hidden-in-plain-view places that's easy to miss.

Despite its location, the plaza is protected from traffic noise by the waterfall that runs along its entire south wall, on the Randolph Street side. The rushing water drowns out the street sounds and also provides a refreshing backdrop on a hot summer day. The water theme is enhanced by an elevated fountain in the center of the plaza, which is surrounded by trees, shrubs, and shade plants. There are plenty of benches scattered throughout the garden; several sit under large glass umbrellas, which provide a canopy in case of a sudden summer rain. There are two street-level elevators just off the sidewalk, for those who can't use the stairs.

The plaza gets crowded during lunch hour in nice weather. But during off-hours, though you may see office workers holding informal meetings or taking smoking breaks, it's generally very quiet. Outdoor tables for patrons of Sopraffina Marketcaffé line the east side of the courtyard, and I've found this a pleasant spot to enjoy a coffee and do some writing on my laptop. If only work could always be so enjoyable.

❋ art institute gardens

chicago's 50 best places to find peace and quiet

ADDRESS: 111 S. Michigan Avenue

Chicago, IL 60603

PHONE: 312-443-3600

ADMISSION: Free

WEBSITE: www.artic.edu

At the Art Institute you have two choices for respite outdoors: a garden on the north side of the building, and one on the south. They're quite different from one another, each with its own particular character.

In the north garden you'll find a large grassy plaza bordered by trees and lavish plantings of native wildflowers. On the eastern side of the lawn run long, parallel rows of ornamental grasses, Siberian irises, and daylilies, designed to evoke the marshy shoreline of a prairie river. There are lots of benches for sitting and gazing at the sculptures by Henry Moore, Alexander Calder, and Ellsworth Kelly as visitors wander through snapping pictures. "Quiet" is a relative term here: Though you can still hear buses as they pass by on Michigan Avenue, you nevertheless get a sense of being off the beaten path.

On the southern side of the building is a sunken garden that I like even better. It's shadier and quieter, with a more formal feel. A huge rectangular fountain in the center is surrounded by two dozen square planters, each holding a low-hanging hawthorn tree ringed with flowers. Separated by gravel pathways, the planters have broad edges wide enough to sit on.

With the canopy of branches so close overhead, the feel is both intimate and spacious—a little like being in a tree house.

On the east side of the garden is an enormous sculpture created by Lorado Taft in 1913, *Fountain of the Great Lakes*. Taft's inspiration for the fountain came from architect Daniel Burnham, who in 1893 criticized local artists charged with ornamenting the fairgrounds of the World's Columbian Exhibition, an internationally renowned fair held in Chicago to commemorate the four hundredth anniversary of Columbus's arrival in the Americas. Burnham lambasted the artists for not drawing enough inspiration from the natural resources of "the West," especially the five Great Lakes. Taft took that criticism and turned it into one of his best-known works: five strong, graceful women holding shells through which water flows in the same order it passes through the Great Lakes system. The water creates a soothing sound that sets a lovely tone for the garden.

If you come before 3 p.m. between late May and early fall, you have another delightful outdoor option: the Garden Restaurant. Enter the museum on the east side, so you can take the stairs down to the lower level without having to pay admission. The restaurant is situated in an outdoor courtyard in the heart of the museum, anchored by Carl Milles's *Triton Fountain* at the center, with umbrella tables surrounding it. The menu is small but adequate, running about $10 to $15 for most dishes, and $7 for a glass of wine. The best time to come is around 2 p.m., so you miss the big lunchtime rush. But even when it's crowded, this is one of the most pleasant and civilized spots to enjoy our all-too-brief summer.

✳ bahá'í house of worship

ADDRESS: 100 Linden Avenue

Wilmette, IL 60091

PHONE: 847-853-2300

HOURS: Daily, 7 a.m. to 6:30 p.m.

ADMISSION: Free

WEBSITE: www.us.bahai.org

I've been to the Taj Mahal, so I can say from firsthand experience that we have an architectural marvel to closely rival that famed Indian mausoleum right here in Chicago: the Bahá'í House of Worship in Wilmette.

Founded in the mid-1800s in Persia, the Bahá'í faith is built on the belief in utter peace and unity—that we are all flowers in the same garden. This vision is reflected in the design of both the temple and the gorgeous gardens surrounding it. "House" doesn't do this exquisite place justice. This is a soaring white temple, made of a gleaming mixture of white concrete and quartz cut into delicate tracery that covers the breathtaking dome inside and out. Because the Bahá'í don't accept contributions from anyone outside the faith, it took 40 years to build and was finally completed in 1953.

Extensive formal plantings and fountains radiate from the nine sides of the temple, which corresponds to the number of world religions represented in the lacy scrolls decorating the dome. If you're ever lucky enough to fly over the temple, you'll see that it's designed to look like a giant blooming lotus on the shore of Lake Michigan, the lotus being a symbol of creation.

Wandering the temple grounds can be a spiritual experience, in the sense that it makes you feel connected to something larger than yourself, whether it's nature or the humanity represented by the international array of people who visit the temple. "It is incumbent on you to be even as one soul, to walk with the same feet," exhorted the prophet of the Bahá'í faith. If everyone were to visit the House of Worship, we all just might be a little more peaceful and compassionate toward one another.

❖ bloch cancer survivors plaza

chicago's 50 best places to find peace and quiet

ADDRESS: Grant Park, at the corner of Randolph Street
and Lake Shore Drive

ADMISSION: Free

If you drive north on Lake Shore Drive past Monroe Harbor, you may have wondered about the two 40-foot-tall granite columns off to the side in Grant Park. They're sentries for the entrance to the Richard & Annette Bloch Cancer Survivors Plaza, a pretty and often practically deserted corner of Grant Park.

The plaza is the work of the R.A. Bloch Cancer Foundation, created after Richard Bloch, co-founder of H & R Block, was diagnosed with terminal lung cancer in 1978. Bloch refused to accept a death sentence and waged an ultimately successful two-year battle against the disease. The foundation has funded parks in nearly two dozen U.S. cities, each meant to represent the idea that a cancer diagnosis should not be synonymous with death.

This plaza-within-a-park is the foundation's largest, most visible green space to date, and it's simply lovely, with a classical, airy feeling, rather like a Greek temple. On the Randolph Street side, a wrought-iron gazebo stands at the top of a broad stairway leading down to the plaza. This large, grassy rectangle is lined on both sides with an ample number of benches and pedestals topped with flower-planted urns. The plaza benefits from its proximity to the much-celebrated Millennium Park because the park siphons off visitors, often leaving this wide, green oasis empty.

I was disproportionately pleased one giddy, early-spring afternoon when the only other person here was a woman who'd lugged her own beach chair out and sat reading in the sun. Now there's a kindred spirit, I thought to myself, someone who knows how to have a good time.

The Bloch Cancer Foundation has plans to build similar parks in every North American city that has a million or more residents. What a great idea—spreading peace and quiet to the masses.

❊ chicago botanic garden

ADDRESS: 1000 Lake Cook Road

Glencoe, IL 60022

PHONE: 847-835-5440

HOURS: 8 a.m. to sunset, every day except Christmas

ADMISSION: Free, but parking is $10 per car, $5.75 for

senior citizens on Tuesday

WEBSITE: www.chicagobotanic.org

I've encountered many Chicagoans who swear that the Botanic Garden is, hands down, the best place in the area to rejuvenate, and it's hard to argue with that claim. Despite being one of the most-visited public gardens in the country, it's so vast that even on a busy day you can still escape far from the madding crowd. With 23 specialty gardens and three native habitat areas spread over 385 acres, this is a nature lover's nirvana.

At the outer reaches of the western edge is one of the less visited areas, the Native Prairie. Late summer and early fall are dazzling. Native grasses stretch as high as eight feet, and thousands of shooting star, joe-pye weed, and starry campion bloom like crazy. With 15 acres to roam, you can commune with the butterflies and honeybees, or watch herons stalk their prey along the edges of the lagoons.

Evening Island is another spot where you can nourish your soul with vibrant natural beauty. The five-acre garden combines perennial flowers and ornamental grasses with trees and shrubs, giving it a designed-but-still-wild feeling.

One of the happiest sights after a Chicago winter occurs here in the spring, when the island's sweeping hillside comes alive with a blanket of yellow daffodils. There are so many great views here, from the Nautilus, a shell-shaped terrace, to the curvaceous Serpentine footbridge that connects the island to the western side of the lake in which it sits.

Other gardens that I love are the Zen-like Japanese Garden, the Waterfall Garden, and the lush and colorful Sensory Garden. After you visit, you may disagree with my picks, but that's the great thing about the Botanic Garden—there's truly something for everyone.

❊ canoeing the chicago river
(at chicago river canoe & kayak)

chicago's 50 best places to find peace and quiet

ADDRESS: Clark Park, east bank of the river (3400 N.
Rockwell)

PHONE: 773-704-2663

HOURS: May through September, Friday, 1 p.m. to sunset; Saturday and Sunday, 9 a.m. to sunset

COST: Canoes and single kayaks, $14 per hour; tandem
kayaks, $18 per hour; no additional charge after four
or more hours

WEBSITE: www.chicagoriverpaddle.com

If you're anything like my husband, you may have lived your
entire life (or a good portion of it) in the city and never once
considered canoeing the Chicago River. I'm guessing that
most city folks just don't realize that an experience associated
with the great outdoors is available to them. It may not be the
same as paddling, say, the Boundary Waters, but an afternoon on the river can give you a whole new view of the city.

For $14 an hour, you can rent a canoe from Chicago River
Canoe & Kayak, which is basically a shed and a tent in Clark
Park (on the east side of the river, on Rockwell between Belmont and Addison). The beginning of the journey is pretty
industrial, with views of warehouses and chugging, clanging
sounds filling the air. But around Berteau Avenue, the river-
banks become much more residential and quieter. You'll
glimpse attractive old homes, where many of the owners have
lovingly tended their pieces of the river's edge, taming the

steep banks with terraces and landscaping. Some residents have decks and docks right on the water, making it easy to get lost in a daydream of another life in which you have a river running right outside your door.

Here in the heart of the city you might think the waterway would be strewn with garbage. While it's by no means pristine, the river actually is remarkably trash-free, and clean enough to allow some wildlife to thrive. We've seen families of ducks and geese, woodchucks, turtles, and fish literally leaping out of the water. Other paddlers have reported seeing foxes, mink, otters, muskrats, and a slew of birds.

As you paddle, you'll pass under quaint-looking bridges at Irving Park and Lawrence. If you're lucky, you'll get to see the El cross the river, suddenly shooting out from behind one tree-shrouded side of the river, then just as quickly disappearing behind the other. It's a picturesque scene, a pleasing combination of the urban and the natural. If you continue paddling to Legion Park, at Peterson, you can turn around and head home knowing you traveled a full three miles from your starting point. The current will help carry you back to the livery, so you can take it easy on the return trip. This will give you ample opportunity to revel in a feeling of smugness; after all, you've enjoyed a view of the city that many other Chicagoans have never seen.

❊ felician sisters grotto

ADDRESS: 3800 W. Peterson Avenue

Chicago, IL 60659

PHONE: 773-463-3020

HOURS: Daily, until sunset

ADMISSION: Free

When my father-in-law, Frank, was a boy growing up in Rogers Park in the 1930s, a visit to the Felician Sisters Grotto provided many an evening's outing for his large family. His father would pack the five oldest kids into the family Buick, then turn them loose on the grounds of this Catholic nuns' convent. Though Frank recalls that he and his siblings tried to behave reverentially, I like to imagine them frisking about, enjoying the feeling of wide-open space as dusk descended on a warm summer evening.

A grotto is a cave constructed of concrete and often adorned with glass, stones, shells, and other objects. The building of grottoes is thought to have originated in the Middle Ages, when shepherds sought out natural caves for shelter; they adorned the grottoes with crucifixes and holy pictures, creating hidden sanctuaries in the hills. During the same period, survivors of various plagues began a tradition of building similar grottoes as a way to thank God for sparing them. European priests, mainly from Germany, brought this tradition to the United States in the 1800s, and because they tended to settle in places like Wisconsin and Iowa, the Midwest now is home to the world's largest concentration of grottoes. These man-made caves are actually considered an important type of folk art, because they are generally built by people with no formal training in art or architecture.

The Felician Sisters grotto provides a unique spot for quiet contemplation, whether or not you have religious leanings. Though the sign on the main gate warns, "No trespassing," the sisters assure me it's fine to visit. Park in the lot at the eastern edge of the property, then follow the walking path toward the back of the expansive, shady lawn, where you'll find the grotto, a large free-form cave created of stone and concrete.

Tucked into an alcove at the top of the grotto, a statue of the Virgin Mary watches over a small waterfall splashing down the rocks to a shallow pool below. You'll often find a vase of fresh flowers nearby, an offering to the Blessed Mother. Kneelers are built into the grotto so you can pray if you wish. I like to sit on a bench off to the side, enjoying the sound of trickling water and breathing in the scent of the flowers and greenery that blanket the surroundings.

Behind the grotto is a paved walking path. Follow it through the stone archway, and you'll find that it winds past stone monuments depicting the Stations of the Cross, donated by different Catholic parishes around the city. The path leads around to the front of the property, to a beautiful little pond with an island in the center, a tiny bridge, and a fountain, all built of the same concrete as the grotto. Unfortunately, this oasis borders Peterson Avenue, so it's not all that quiet, but it nevertheless is a feast for the eyes. If it's raining, you can still enjoy the view from the shelter of the charming weather-beaten Victorian-style gazebo off to the side. Wherever you are, the grotto provides the kind of spiritual experience that anyone can appreciate, no matter what their religion.

❋ fermilab

ADDRESS: Wilson and Kirk Roads

Batavia, IL 60510

PHONE: 630-840-3000

HOURS: Mid-October to mid-April, open daily from

 8 a.m. to 6 p.m.; mid-April to mid-October, open daily

 from 8 a.m. to 8 p.m.

ADMISSION: Free

WEBSITE: www.fnal.gov

NOTE: The public may use the Batavia Road and Pine

 Street entrances; see website for map.

Why am I recommending that you go to the trouble of driving an hour or more to the outer reaches of Chicago-land to visit, of all things, a high-energy physics lab? Because Fermilab is surrounded by hundreds of acres of open land where you can bike, hike, cross-country ski, canoe, ice-skate, and commune with all kinds of wildlife, including a herd of buffalo—yes, buffalo.

One of six National Environmental Research Parks in the country, Fermilab is unique in that it comprises nearly all the major ecosystems of the Midwest, from woodlands to wetlands. This is a fantastic place to spend the day reveling in the kind of wide-open space that used to characterize this part of the country.

The herd of about 45 buffalo is one of the main attractions here, though it's strictly an urban legend that they're used as mammalian Geiger counters to warn of radioactive danger. Actually, they're descendents of the buffalo originally brought to the grounds by the lab's first director, who wanted to strengthen Fermilab's connection to its prairie surroundings. Where else in Chicago are you going to see buffalo at home on the range?

Following 9/11, Fermilab was off-limits to the public, but the Department of Energy loosened the restrictions in early 2005, and once again most of the recreation areas are open for anyone to enjoy. Still, it's a good idea to check the website's "Visiting Fermilab" page before you make the trip.

❊ fourth presbyterian church courtyard

ADDRESS: 866 N. Michigan Avenue (the main entrance to the sanctuary is around the corner, at 126 E. Chestnut)
Chicago, IL 60611
PHONE: 312-787-4570
ADMISSION: Free
WEBSITE: www.fourthchurch.org

Fourth Presbyterian Church is one of those famous old Chicago buildings that you may have guessed has a fascinating history; you just don't know what it is. Well, here's an interesting nugget: After two years of planning and construction, the Fourth Presbyterian congregation dedicated its first church on October 8, 1871. Does that date sound familiar? One can assume that the young congregation's joy rapidly turned to horror, because the Great Chicago Fire burned the church to the ground the very day it was dedicated.

Eventually, in 1914, the congregation built the present incarnation of Fourth Presbyterian on Michigan Avenue. It's the oldest building on the avenue, and to me it has always seemed a little out of place. Its ivy-covered walls and Gothic Revival style seem more suited to one of Chicago's quiet neighborhood side streets than this bustling, skyscraper-lined thoroughfare. But when the church was built, what was to become the Magnificent Mile was just a quiet road called Pine Street. As the neighborhood grew up (and up and up) during the last century, the church has become a refuge in an otherwise busy area of the city.

When the madness of the Mile gets too overwhelming, duck into the church's courtyard. Encircled on all sides by ivy-covered walls, it's a cool, green spot to pause and take a breather. You won't find any benches here, but stone stairways in two of the corners are pleasant spots to sit. From here you can admire the Gothic stone archways lining the airy cloister on the eastern side, the stained glass windows of the sanctuary, and the fountain in the middle of the grassy courtyard.

❊ graceland cemetery

ADDRESS: 4001 N. Clark Street

Chicago, IL 60613

PHONE: 773-525-1105

HOURS: Daily, 8 a.m. to 4:30 p.m.

ADMISSION: Free

WEBSITE: www.gracelandcemetery.org

Chicago is home to many notable cemeteries, but Graceland is unquestionably one of the prettiest. Unlike the stark burial grounds that preceded it, Graceland, established in 1860, was designed by landscape architects who wanted to create a natural, parklike setting. They most certainly succeeded.

Covering a generous 119 bucolic acres between Irving Park and Montrose at Clark Street, Graceland is a place where you can find ample solitary space any time of year. I particularly like the fall. Pay a visit around mid-October and you'll be rewarded with the sight of full flaming autumnal color from the massive oaks, elms, maples, and the variety of shrubs that cover the grounds.

Dozens of Chicago luminaries have found their eternal rest at Graceland, and you could spend days wandering around, gaping at the opulent monuments which their wealth enabled them to build. Marshall Field lies below a Grecian-style statue called *Memory*, designed by the men who went on to create the Lincoln Memorial. William Kimball, the piano manufacturer, has one of the largest monuments here, a striking white marble structure with Corinthian columns. Peter

Schoenhofen, owner of Schoenhofen Brewery, rests under an Egyptian-style pyramid complete with sphinx.

One of my favorite spots is Lake Willomere, in the northeast section. Cross the concrete bridge at the north end, and you'll find yourself on a small island, where famed city planner Daniel Burnham and his family are buried. Headstones made of granite boulders make a nice spot to sit and contemplate the leaf-dappled pond; two enormous weeping willows and other greenery ring the island, giving it a very private feel.

If you want to check out other beautiful cemeteries, **Oak Woods** (1035 E. 67th Street) and **Rosehill** (5800 N. Ravenswood) also feature truly amazing funerary art. When you visit any of these cemeteries, please keep in mind that, pastoral as they are, they're burial grounds, not parks. Pets, picnics, and recreational activities are not permitted.

(The Chicago Architecture Foundation offers walking tours of Graceland, Oak Woods, and Rosehill cemeteries. Visit the foundation's website at www.architecture.org, or call 312-922-3432.)

❃ the green at grant park

ADDRESS: 352 E. Monroe Street

Chicago, IL 60603

PHONE: 312-642-7888

HOURS: April through October, open daily

10 a.m. to 10 p.m.

COST: For golf, $8 for 18 holes, $6.50 for nine holes. (No

charge for relaxing.)

WEBSITE: www.thegreenonline.com

It had been a while since I had ventured all the way out to the lake by way of Monroe Street, so I was quite astonished one day to find that this busy street has become home to a kind of secret garden in plain view.

The setting is the Green at Grant Park, which at first glance appears to be a remarkably nice miniature-golf course, with verdant, well-manicured greens the size of those at a putt-putt but without any amusement-park kitsch cluttering each hole. Step a little closer, though, inside the wrought-iron fence that frames it, and you'll discover a grown-up putting course meant to challenge even the most serious player.

Honestly, though, I couldn't care less about golf. What draws me here are the beautiful gardens surrounding the course. You might expect the plantings to be fussy and formal, but they're quite the opposite: The grassy paths connecting the putting greens gracefully wind their way among terraced hills edged with limestone slabs. Set among the many trees are informal plantings of perennials: spiky purple catmint, coral bells, native grasses, pink spirea bushes, Stella d'Oro lilies blooming like crazy. With the many trees providing a canopy of shade, the feeling is of being in a woodland garden.

Here in Chicago—heck, the entire Midwest—our eyes get so used to flatness that it's a rare treat to be able to rest them on some hills, especially such lushly planted ones. You do notice the traffic a bit, but I've found there's a rhythm to it, the drone of cars punctuated by quiet lulls when the traffic lights change. Apart from that, the only thing you'll hear are the birds. The combination of the iron fence lining the street side and the terraced hills protecting the back side provide a strong sense that the rest of the world is out *there*.

If you're hungry, you can enjoy the view of the gardens from the café, which has tables set around a wide concrete patio. The cabana-style restaurant offers a decent selection of soups, appetizers, salads, and sandwiches; prices range from about $8 to $12.

I've found the most restful way to soak up the setting is to procure a cool drink from the café, then take it out to a shady spot in the gardens, settling either on the roomy stone steps on the north side of the course or the shady bench to the south, between the 11th and 15th holes. Play on through if you like. I'll just be taking it easy.

❋ humboldt park boathouse and formal garden

ADDRESS: 1359 N. Humboldt Drive (Sacramento Avenue

    becomes Humboldt Drive between Augusta Boulevard

    and North Avenue)

Chicago, IL 60622

ADMISSION: Free

When someone in the city planning department recommended I check out the Humboldt Park Boathouse, my first
thought was, "Yeah, right. Maybe with a bodyguard." My main
experience with the area had been back in the early 1990s,
when I had a starving-activist-type boyfriend who lived near
the gang-infested park. One night a cabbie dropped me off at
his apartment with the warning, "Girl, I hope you got an Uzi."
Not exactly an image that summons up visions of serenity.

My source assured me I'd be safe, so one hot morning I
ventured out to the park. What a revelation. Since the late
1990s, the Chicago Park District has invested a fortune into ren-
ovating Humboldt Park, and it's paid off. The gangs that once
roamed this 207-acre verdant area have been replaced by families with young children (during the day at least).

One of the main attractions is the Prairie-style boathouse,
an open-air pavilion originally built in 1907. Widely acclaimed
in architectural journals of the day, it was a popular spot for
fishing, boating, picnics, concerts, and, in the winter, ice-skat-
ing. During the 1960s and 1970s, though, the surrounding
neighborhood went into decline, and the boathouse fell victim

to vandalism and graffiti. The renovations, however, have restored the boathouse to its former glory, complete with plantings based on old postcards of the boathouse.

There are also some nice contemporary touches. Befitting Humboldt Park's setting in the heart of the city's Puerto Rican community, one side of the boathouse is now home to **La Palma in the Park**, a Puerto Rican restaurant selling inexpensive traditional fare (pork dishes are a specialty). In nice weather, the restaurant puts tables out on the boathouse's spacious veranda, which overlooks a large, placid lagoon.

From the boathouse, you can meander around the lagoon on a gravel walking path lined with trees, marsh grasses, and wildflowers. Every few paces, the path branches off to stone ledges right on the water, where you can sit and gaze at the clusters of men and children (and the rare woman) casting fishing lines into the water, like a scene from an Impressionist painting. Along the eastern side, look for the big stone snail engraved with the exhortation, "Breathe Oxygen."

The most stunning part of Humboldt Park, though, is the Formal Garden, across the street from the boathouse, at the northwest corner of Humboldt Boulevard and Division Street. The garden is positively breathtaking—like a bit of Versailles on the West Side. Huge flower beds in shades of lime green, purple, red, orange, and bronze encircle a center fountain that you actually can walk through (be careful though; the mossy ground is slippery). Pavilions on three sides offer a place to sit and drink in the sight of all this beauty and to enjoy the heady aroma from huge swaths of basil. It's heartening to see that Chicago's reputation for beautiful plantings isn't reserved just for heavily touristed areas; this is definitely a neighborhood spot, one you'll want to visit again and again.

☀ ice-skating at daley bicentennial plaza

ADDRESS: 337 E. Randolph Street

Chicago, IL 60611

PHONE: 312-742-7648

HOURS: From the day after Thanksgiving through mid-March, weather depending, Monday through Friday, 10 a.m. to 4 p.m. and 7 to 9:30 p.m.; Saturday and Sunday, 8:30 a.m. to noon

ADMISSION: Free, with your own skates; skate rental is $4

Why is it that so many of us loved to ice-skate as children but so rarely do it as adults? Strapping on a pair of skates for an hour or two is one of the best ways I know to recapture that sense of freedom and unlimited time that was so easy to access as a child, and yet is so hard to find as an adult.

Daley Bicentennial Plaza has long been a great place to skate outdoors without huge crowds, and it's become even more so since the rink at nearby Millennium Park opened to much fanfare in 2004. Daley Plaza does get crowded around Christmas, when schoolkids are on winter break, but except for those two weeks or so, you'll have plenty of room to spin. Heck, if you come when it opens at 8:30 on the weekend, you may even have the rink to yourself.

There are several other outdoor rinks around the city. Two of the best are at **Riis Park** (6100 W. Fullerton) and **Warren Park** (6601 N. Western Avenue), where the trees surrounding both rinks give them a secluded, woodsy feel.

❄ indian boundary prairies

ADDRESS: Near the junction of Route 57 and
Interstate 294 in south suburban Markham
(Directions are available online at
www.prairiepages.com/prairie/Cook_Prairie.html#markham)
Overseen by the Nature Conservancy
Chicago Office: 8 S. Michigan Avenue, Suite 900
Chicago, IL 60603
PHONE: 312-580-2100
HOURS: Daily, during daylight hours
ADMISSION: Free

There are a number of restored prairielands around Chicago, where conservationists have taken denuded or overgrown parcels of land and replanted them with grasses and wildflowers native to Illinois. But if you want to see true virgin prairie that's never been cut or marred in any way, head south to Indian Boundary Prairies, in suburban Markham.

Totaling more than three hundred acres, the prairies consist of four separate tracts about 10 minutes apart from each other. Originally slated for housing developments in the 1920s, the prairies were one of the few beneficiaries of the Great Depression, which eliminated the funds for development. The best one to visit is Gensburg-Markham Prairie, which is the largest of the four, with a 1.2-mile trail winding through it. In late summer, when the grasses reach as high as five feet, it's quite something to experience what our pioneer ancestors must have seen when they first encountered the Great Plains. The prairies are especially known for the large number of butterflies that flock here, and it's beautiful to see them flitting among hundreds of blooming prairie flowers.

The peak bloom times are in May, early July, and August. If you go in the heat of summer, keep in mind that there is no shade. Bring a hat or even an umbrella and plenty of water.

✳ the labyrinth at st. james episcopal cathedral

ADDRESS: 56 E. Huron
Chicago, IL 60611
PHONE: 312-787-7360
ADMISSION: Free

I was pretty skeptical the first time I went seeking peace and quiet at the labyrinth behind St. James Episcopal Cathedral, because its location turned out to be not all that peaceful and not all that quiet. The spiraling footpath is painted on the ground in a stark concrete courtyard, and that first time, as I contemplated entering the labyrinth, the air was filled with city sounds: a jackhammer pounding, fire engines blaring, horns honking.

But once I decided to give it a go, to my surprise the process of walking the labyrinth left me feeling calmer and more centered, like it's supposed to.

The labyrinthian form derives from the shape of the spiral, a universal symbol of transformation and growth. No one knows the exact history of labyrinthian spirals, but variations have been found on pottery, tiles, and tablets that are at least four thousand years old. Most likely, they originally mimicked shapes found in nature. Certainly, spiral patterns can be found in a variety of ancient cultures, such as the Native American medicine wheel and the Celts' never-ending circle. What all these forms have in common is that they are not mazes with dead-ends but rather circuitous paths that lead without interruption to the center, then back out.

The labyrinth at St. James is based on the one that was built into the floor of France's Chartres Cathedral during the Crusades in the 13th century, so that those who were unable to make a pilgrimage to Jerusalem could still take a spiritual journey. It is fairly small by labyrinth standards—about 28 feet across. The footpath is designed so you enter and exit at the same point by winding your way around to the center, then winding your way back out.

There are three parts to walking a labyrinth: First, before you begin, pause to clear your mind and call up a question or issue you may be wrestling with, asking for guidance if you like. Next, as you walk in, focus on releasing the worries that weigh you down; when you reach the center, pause and still your mind as much as you're able to for a little while. Finally, as you make your way out, take with you into the world the feelings or insights you gained during your walk.

It isn't always noisy around St. James, but even when it is, I've found that the process of putting one foot in front of the other and simply following the spiral where it leads becomes kind of a walking meditation. The curves are tightly drawn, so you really have to focus as you go. Once you enter the labyrinth, you tend to lose all sense of how close you are to reaching the center or the exit, and it becomes easier, however briefly, to be in the present moment—something a lot of us have a hard time doing. I don't necessarily get a direct answer to the question I may have sent out to the universe as I prepared to enter, but I do tend to leave with a sense of calm, and feeling more centered.

While you're here, check out the *Angel of Peace*, ready to ascend to the heavens from the plaza in front of the Episcopal Church Center, on the northeast side of the labyrinth. Artist Will Kieffer created this bronze sculpture for the 60th anniversary of the Episcopal Peace Fellowship in 1999. The gardens around the statue and along the back of the cathedral are pretty too.

❋ the lakefront path, southern end

chicago's 50 best places to find peace and quiet

ADDRESS: From 12th to 71st Streets

ADMISSION: Free

Chicago has one of the most stunning waterfronts of any city in the world, but ironically, in all the years I lived near Belmont and the lake, I hardly ever ventured over to the lakefront path. The only time I could get there was in the evenings and on the weekends, when it tends to be hopelessly clogged. Pairs of walkers obliviously take up the whole path. Rollerbladers whip by with no warning. Joggers will suddenly take a U-turn and crash into cyclists on their heels. It's madness. A handful of people actually have died from head injuries incurred during collisions on the path.

I'm embarrassed to admit that back then I never thought of exploring the miles of lakefront path between what is now the Museum Campus and 71st Street. After all, that's the big, bad South Side, which, for non-residents, is an area known for its wide swaths of poverty and crime. Apparently, a lot of North Siders are still as fearful as I once was. I actually was on my way to the South Side recently when I heard local comedian Aaron Freeman riffing on public radio about how the diversity of the lakefront path disappears around the McCormick Place waterfall, perhaps because south of here the path becomes less populated with museum visitors and conventioneers.

But if you haven't checked out the southernmost leg of the lakefront path, you're missing out on one of the most gorgeous and serene attractions in the city. Unlike the insanity up north, strolling or riding the path south is completely relaxing. It's never crowded, even on a perfect, cloudless, 70-degree Sunday afternoon in June. And because Lake Shore Drive acts as a buffer between the path and the rest of the city, it's fairly safe.

If you begin heading south on the path at Roosevelt Road (1200 south), you'll have a little more than eight miles of path to explore before reaching the end, at the South Shore Cultural Center. No matter where you are on the path, the view is always stunning. How could it not be, with the lake sparkling to the east the entire length of the path? You can also see the boats at Burnham Harbor (1800 south), the aforementioned waterfall at McCormick Place (2300 south), young hipsters practicing with their boards at the skate park (3200 south), gorgeous Promontory Point (5500 south; see page 105 for entry), the lovely old 63rd Street Beach House, Jackson Park Harbor, and the lushly green South Shore Golf Course, not to mention picnic areas, basketball and tennis courts, beaches, and playgrounds.

If you want to try biking the path, but don't have a bike of your own, you can rent one from **Bike Chicago**, at North Avenue or Navy Pier (www.bikechicago.com).

✱ morton arboretum

ADDRESS: 4100 Illinois, Route 53

    Lisle, IL 60532

PHONE: 630-968-0074

HOURS: Daily, during daylight savings time, 7 a.m. to

    7 p.m.; during central standard time, 7 a.m. to 5 p.m.

ADMISSION: Adults, $5; children 3–12, $2; seniors, $4

WEBSITE: www.mortonarb.org

After years of living in rural Massachusetts, then the paradise of northern California, my friends Anna and Dan landed in Chicago. Adapting to a lifestyle that doesn't include nature right outside their front door hasn't been easy. When they feel the need to escape urban life, they seek refuge on the trails at Morton Arboretum.

The arboretum was founded in 1922 by Joy Morton, the owner of Morton Salt, who came by his love of trees naturally; his father started Arbor Day in 1872, and the family's motto was "Plant Trees." Morton devoted the last 13 years of his life to creating a tree preserve that covered 735 acres of his estate at the time of his death. His heirs continued the work, and today the arboretum comprises 1,700 acres of not only trees but specialty gardens as well. You can hike 14 miles of trails that wind among thousands of trees, breathe in the scent of aromatic plants and flowers in the Fragrance Garden, picnic at the edge of Sterling Pond or Lake Marmo, enjoy a book in the Reading Garden, or get lost in the Maze Garden.

Each season offers its own special pleasures. Fall, of course, is glorious, but the arboretum tends to be mobbed then, especially on October weekends. I also love spring, when the 15-acre Daffodil Glade explodes with more than 100,000 daffodils, jonquils, narcissus, and wildflowers. If you're a member, you can bike the trails during the summer members-only evenings; it's a benefit that makes joining well worthwhile. (Membership starts at $45 and includes other members-only events, such as plant and bulb sales.) And winter is especially lovely here; after a snowfall, you can rent snowshoes to explore the trails. Whenever you visit, this is a place where you can amble for hours, drinking in enough nature to get you through another week (or month) back in the City of Big Shoulders.

✢ north park university campus

ADDRESS: 3225 W. Foster Avenue

Chicago, IL 60625

ADMISSION: Free

WEBSITE: www.northpark.edu

Even though I'm in my 40s, the passing of Labor Day each year still brings feelings of nostalgia for my school days. I mourn the end of summer's sunshine and freedom, but seeing children head back to school for another year's learning never fails to arouse the sense that new beginnings are possible at any age.

When I really want to indulge these feelings, I head to North Park University, a Christian college founded in 1891. Though the campus faces busy Foster Avenue, if you wander behind all the old brick-and-stone buildings, you'll find a sense of serenity befitting a theological institute of higher learning.

At Foster and Spaulding avenues, follow the paved path south for a few hundred yards to the heart of the campus. Paved walkways crisscross grassy lawns edged with huge plantings of native flora. Early October is a gorgeous time to visit, when late-blooming roses and golden shafts of prairie grasses stand in contrast to the backdrop of still-green lawns and changing autumn leaves. Low stone walls and benches provide ample room to sit and read or watch students pass by on their way to class.

The path continues south until it dead-ends at a stream; bear to the left and you'll come upon a comfortable bench, where you can sit with the riverbank and turning trees behind you and a grassy lawn and white-painted gazebo in front of you. I find it's a nice place to contemplate where life has taken me since my college days. I may be middle-aged now, but this lovely little spot takes me back to a time when life was still a book waiting to be written—and reminds me that there are many chapters still to come.

❄ north park village nature center

ADDRESS: 5801 N. Pulaski Road

Chicago, IL 60646

PHONE: 312-744-5472

HOURS: Daily, 10 a.m. to 4 p.m.

ADMISSION: Free

I've often joked that my husband, Matt, is like Dr. Doolittle, with an almost spooky ability to communicate with animals. But I never imagined my daughter and I would see him play hide-and-seek with a deer right here in the city. We had just come around a bend in the main walking trail at the North Park Village Nature Center when we spotted a doe nibbling on greenery about 30 feet away. We expected her to dart away, but instead she simply stood and watched us, poised for flight. We took a few steps closer and still she remained. Then Matt got playful. He ducked his head down, and the deer did the same. He rose up and looked over a branch, and the deer lifted her head. He moved right, she mirrored him by leaning left. And so the game went, until finally we said good-bye and moved on down the trail.

It was a special moment at a special place in the city. North Park Village Nature Center is Chicago's only official nature center, a 46-acre sanctuary comprising woodlands, wetlands, prairie, and savanna—Illinois's original four ecosystems. Wandering the paths here takes me back to my childhood in Ohio, when my sister and I used to play in the woods behind our house. Like the woods of my youth, the trees here aren't very dense, but they provide a refuge with a pronounced sense of privacy.

You can wander the ecosystems by taking one of the two walking loops. Chances are good you'll have the place mainly to yourself, even on a beautiful summer Saturday afternoon. If you take the half-mile main loop, you'll come to a pleasant resting spot on a bench by the main pond. Tall grasses sway in the breeze and you can watch schools of catfish swim lazily among the heaps of lily pads. You can't entirely escape the sound of traffic on nearby Pulaski Road, but you can still enjoy the sounds of the birds as you sit in the cool peace of the shade.

As you come off the wooden trail bridge over the wetland area, the trail splits in three directions. Go straight ahead, up the hill, and you'll arrive at one of the nicest spots in the center, where the top of the hill overlooks a sun-dappled grove. Here, before the hillside becomes too overgrown in high summer, you can see much of the sanctuary at once while you sit and do nothing but listen to the sound of the wind in the trees. Perhaps you'll contemplate the wildlife you've seen during your hike—a great blue heron, painted turtles, or ducks swimming together. When you're ready to move on, make your way back to the main building, where you'll find several picnic tables scattered among the trees behind it—a nice place to enjoy a snack and a drink (pack your own; the center doesn't sell any).

Before heading home, be sure to walk about a block east of the parking lot to see the beautiful pond surrounded by rocky ledges, waterfalls, and prairie plants. The trail that winds around behind the waterfalls is another great place to forget you live in the city.

osaka garden
(on wooded island in jackson park)

ADDRESS: 5800 S. Lake Shore Drive

PHONE: 773-256-0903

HOURS: Daily, 8 a.m. to 11 p.m.

ADMISSION: Free

NOTE: Parking is available in the free lot on East Science
Drive (off Lake Shore Drive, just south of 57th Drive).
From the lot, follow the sign with the symbol of the
pagoda, bearing south on the footpath and crossing
the bridge to Wooded Island.

Of the more than 80 suggestions I received for peaceful places
in the city, by far the most frequently mentioned was Osaka
Garden. Indeed, this sanctuary near the Museum of Science
and Industry turned out to be one of my favorite spots.

Osaka Garden was originally built in 1893 for the World's
Columbian Exhibition (see entry for Art Institute Gardens on
page 64). In 1973, the cities of Osaka and Chicago became
"sister cities," and signed an agreement to promote cultural
and educational exchanges between them. One of the even-
tual outcomes of the agreement was the renovation of the
garden, which had fallen into disrepair since its creation.

Intended to provide a tranquil spot for meditation, Osaka
Garden is a traditional Japanese hillside strolling garden,
designed so that visitors can't view the entire garden from a
single vantage point. The formal wooden entrance gate, a gift
from Osaka's Mayor Nishio in 1994, is a wonderful piece of

craftsmanship, made without a single nail by using the tongue-and-groove method. Following the meandering gravel path from the gate guides you to ever-changing vistas meant to refresh and stimulate your senses. The composition of the garden's elements—rocks, a gurgling waterfall and still pond, hills, graceful plantings, granite lanterns—is deliberately asymmetrical, yet somehow feels perfectly balanced. The effect is beautifully harmonious and serene.

One of my favorite parts of the garden is the Moon Bridge, which crosses the pond. Does your soul feel lighter as you cross the bridge? By taking this curved path over the water, one is thought to shed evil spirits, which travel only in straight lines and fall into the pond below as you walk. Fed by a waterfall at its south end, the pond is ringed with large stones and manicured plantings. As you stroll around the pond, you may run into Bill Coons, the man largely responsible for the garden's beauty. Bill spent seven years as a volunteer at Osaka Garden before the park district finally put him on the payroll in 2001. Now he spends about two hundred hours a year lovingly tending the Zen-like landscape. I was surprised to learn from Bill that though it feels thoroughly Japanese, the garden contains mainly North American plants. Native Japanese plants wouldn't survive Chicago's harsh climate, so Bill gives local ones a traditional Japanese appearance by pruning them to create open spaces, flat planes, and an aged effect—an art he learned firsthand from a great Japanese garden designer, Sadafumiu Uchiyama.

Near the waterfall is a traditional Japanese teahouse, a raised, covered pavilion with attached benches all around the outer edges. No one sells tea here, but you can certainly bring a thermos of your own, which is a pleasant thing to do on a gloomy, but not-too-chilly, fall day. You'll most likely be left entirely alone to sip your tea in the shelter of the pavilion. Drink in the serenity of the garden and the flaming colors of the trees blanketing Jackson Park, which surrounds Wooded Island. The tranquility of this scene might actually leave you looking forward to a gray day.

✳ promontory point

ADDRESS: 5491 S. Lake Shore Drive

Chicago, IL 60615

PHONE: 312-742-4838

ADMISSION: Free

As at so many of Chicago's most beautiful outdoor places, the imprint of famed Prairie School landscape designer Alfred Caldwell is all over Promontory Point, a large peninsula jutting into Lake Michigan. Caldwell saw this space as the meeting point between the vast midwestern prairie and the Great Lakes, and he wanted to create a place that, as he said, delighted visitors with "a sense of space and a sense of the power of nature and the power of the sea." Using funds and labor from the Works Progress Administration, he created a circular park that protrudes into the lake, providing panoramic views of the water, shoreline, and city.

The centerpiece of the point is an enormous grassy meadow ringed by a thick band of trees: elms, American lindens, prairie crabapples, sugar maples, American hop hornbeams, hawthorns, and pines. At the top of the circular meadow's eastern slope is an enchanting stone field house that looks like a castle. And encircling the entire point is a wonderful paved path dotted with several of Caldwell's signature "council rings"—low stone circles for gathering around and even building fires in the center.

At the far edge of the point, right on the water, is a revetment, four levels of limestone slabs that provide ample room for lying in the sun and contemplating the vastness of the lake. This revetment is at the heart of a battle over Promontory Point, launched in 2001 when the city announced plans to replace the slabs with a concrete structure as part of its massive project to rebuild several miles of eroded shoreline. Activists were incensed and managed to stall the project. As of this writing the two sides were still negotiating, but prospects looked good for a design that would preserve the original character of the Point.

No matter when you visit, Promontory Point is gorgeous—in spring when the leaves first unfurl; in summer, when cooling lake breezes blow; in fall, when the thickets of trees flame with color; or in winter, when snow blankets the trees. Just call it serenity for all seasons.

❈ riverbank neighbors

ADDRESS: East bank of the Chicago River between
Berteau and Montrose
WEBSITE: www.BeyondToday.com/river
ADMISSION: Free

On the northwest side of the city is a riverside trail where, if you use your imagination, you just might find yourself in touch with the spirit of Huck Finn. Here on the banks of the Chicago River, thickets of trees grow right to the river's edge, their reflection in the water casting a deep green light everywhere. A family of geese drifts languidly downstream, quizzically approaching visitors for food. The air is perfumed by the scent of the woods, a rare olfactory treat in the city.

Even if this weren't such a tranquil spot, I'd have to love it for the spirit of community and devotion to nature it embodies. Back in the mid-1990s, the east bank of the river between Berteau and Montrose was blighted by soil erosion, illegal dumping, and hoodlums hanging out. Some schoolchildren decided to beautify the area by planting a thatch of Virginia bluebells. The students' efforts galvanized what became a neighborhood mission to reclaim the riverbank. Neighbors got together and hauled away garbage and discarded chunks of concrete, cut back overgrown vegetation, and planted ground cover to hold the soil in place. They cut terraces into the riverbank to stop further erosion, and most wonderful of all, they created a woodchip trail lined with a rustic fence fashioned from tree branches and brush.

Today, those original bluebells still bloom, along with columbine, bloodroot, wild ginger, trout lilies, May apples, celadine poppies, and prairie trillium. It's become a cool, green place of beauty known as Riverbank Neighbors, and it's open to everyone. The trail isn't very long, but it has several places for respite: a small dock where you can launch a canoe or kayak, several stairways that have been cut into the bank and reinforced with timber, a couple of places where you can bring a beach chair and sit along the trail. On a hot summer day, this is a relaxing place to soak up some shade and maybe even enjoy a cool breeze off the river.

Be sure to wear sturdy shoes when you visit—the trail is steep in a couple of spots. If you want to pitch in and help the volunteers who so lovingly tend this urban patch of nature, visit the website for information. The community welcomes assistance from honorary "neighbors."

✳ riverwalk

When the din of Michigan Avenue gets to be too much, escape by taking the curving staircase at 401 N. Michigan (by the double-decker bus tours stand) down to the Riverwalk. Stretching from Michigan Avenue all the way to Lake Shore Drive, this series of connecting plazas is a restful place where you can relax and watch the river flow.

The most pleasant part of Riverwalk is the stretch below the University of Chicago Graham School of General Studies. Nicely landscaped with trees and shrubbery, this section provides ample shade in warm weather and loads of benches for reading or quiet contemplation. If you keep going under the Columbus Drive Bridge, past the Sheraton, and on to McClurg Court, you'll arrive at the spectacular Centennial Fountain and Water Arc, which is active from May 1 through September 30. Look for the cement column holding a one-hundred-year time capsule, to be unearthed June 30, 2089.

All along the Riverwalk you'll find several places to stop for coffee or a snack. If you're brown-bagging it, you might prefer the south side of the river, which you can access on the south side of the bridge at Michigan Avenue. Being just below Lower Wacker Drive and its steady traffic, it's not as quiet and has far fewer benches—but that just means that it's even less peopled, and it has plenty of grassy spots for a picnic.

The Riverwalk is lovely in the evening, when even on a sweltering summer night you can catch a breeze as the lights of the city come up. But don't forget about the path in the winter. The river is an especially compelling sight when it's frozen in snow-covered chunks, looking like a giant meringue confection in the heart of downtown.

❋ secret garden café

ADDRESS: 6219 N. Sheridan Road, in Berger Park

Chicago, IL 60660

PHONE: 773-381-5623 (in season)

HOURS: Memorial Day to Labor Day, Sunday through

    Thursday, 11 a.m. to 9 p.m.; Friday and

    Saturday, 11 a.m. to 10 p.m.

NOTE: Open until 7 p.m. only during inclement weather

Chicago offers many, many places to dine al fresco, but I'd be willing to bet that not one has as lovely a view as the Secret Garden Café. Hugging the rocks that border the shore at Berger Park, this adorable eatery has a completely unobstructed view of the lake. Sit on the patio on a cloudless day, and you'll see nothing but sun-drenched, blue-green water all the way to the horizon.

The café is a little hard to find unless you know where to look. Tucked behind the North Lakeside Cultural Arts Center, it's accessible through a sweet little wrought-iron archway and surrounded by trees and shade-loving plants. The patio is small—about a dozen or so tables—and attracts a crowd for weekend brunch. It's not worth going if you have to sit inside on a sunny day—the atmosphere is dim and not that attractive. But on a rainy day, the indoors has a certain appeal. The glassed-in porch blocks the view of the rocks, and it's easy to imagine you're cozy and snug in a boat right on the water.

The offerings are billed as "meals and snacks that feel like a picnic in the park," and I have to agree. The food is fresh and good, and tends toward the lighter side—mainly salads and sandwiches. I haven't tried the desserts, but people rave about them. It's like a picnic without preparation: just show up, order your food, and enjoy the view.

❊ seneca park

ADDRESS: 228 E. Chicago Avenue
Chicago, IL 60611
PHONE: 312-742-7891
ADMISSION: Free

Like all great cities, Chicago attracts a lot of visitors, especially in the summer. During the week, Michigan Avenue can become overwhelmingly crowded with a combination of locals on lunch break and out-of-towners admiring the sites. Fortunately, just a block away from the chaos surrounding the shopping mecca Water Tower Place, there's a relatively undiscovered escape: Seneca Park.

Located just south of Water Tower, between Chicago and Peterson at Mies van der Rohe Way, Seneca is a shady little refuge with the feel of an old-fashioned city park. A wrought-iron fence surrounds tree-lined brick pathways, wooden benches, and quaint street lamps. You will undoubtedly encounter a few homeless people here, but usually I find they're just looking for a place to sleep, not money, and I'm left undisturbed. It's really a lovely, peaceful spot to eat a brown-bag lunch al fresco and read a book.

Before you leave, be sure to have a look at *Ben*, a horse constructed of sticks by Montana sculptor Deborah Butterfield.

✳ south shore cultural center nature sanctuary

ADDRESS: 7059 S. Shore Drive

Chicago, IL 60649

PHONE: 773-256-0149

HOURS: Daily, until sunset

ADMISSION: Free

WEBSITE: www.chicagoparkdistrict.com

Of all the tranquil spots I've found in Chicago, the nature sanctuary at the South Shore Cultural Center feels the most like being outside the city. You practically are, really—the downtown skyline rises like Shangri-la in the distance, more than eight miles away. Also, the topography is different here, with natural sand dunes that are extremely unusual for the Chicago shoreline. Down here, I'm able to tap into the same feeling of calm that I usually experience only when escaping to Michigan for a quiet weekend at the beach.

The four-acre sanctuary exists thanks to the efforts of community activists, who had long advocated for a nature center on the peninsula just beyond the southern end of the Cultural Center's beach. Their dreams were realized in 2001, when the Chicago Park District began construction of this area that encompasses not just dunes but also a small wetland and large prairie landscape. The beauty of the sanctuary was recognized in 2002 with an award from the Environmental Protection Agency and Chicago Wilderness (a coalition of groups dedicated to conservation) for best conservation and native landscaping.

The sanctuary is an important resting and feeding spot for migrating birds. It's especially pretty in the fall, when you can follow the concrete path from the entrance to a boardwalk that winds past the dunes and over the wetland area, and leads to a marshy pond surrounded by brilliant autumn foliage. You can pause on one of the benches here or continue up the hill, past a large butterfly meadow, where you'll come to two limestone "council rings," a hallmark of legendary Prairie School landscape architect Jens Jensen and his protégé Alfred Caldwell. The rings are meant to be a place for small gatherings and storytelling. One of them is just above the lake, and the other is several yards inland. Pausing here is a multisensory experience, with the view of the city in the distance, the sound of rushing waves below, and the scent of past campfires lingering in the air. Continuing on the path will lead you through a prairie environment, but I tend not to go any farther. I like to sit here on the very edge of the land, drinking in the view and the sound of the surf, and feeling like I can truly be all alone in the city.

✳ 12th street beach

chicago's 50 best places to find peace and quiet

ADDRESS: 12th Street and the Lake

PHONE: 312-742-5121

HOURS: Daily, Memorial Day weekend through Labor
Day weekend, 9 a.m. to 9 p.m.

ADMISSION: Free

On a hot, sticky day, when you feel like a dip in the lake but don't want to fight the crowds, try the 12th Street Beach. Despite its proximity to one of the most heavily touristed parts of the city, it's rarely crowded, and since Mayor Daley shut down nearby Meigs Field airport in 2003, it's quiet now too.

The beach is just south of Adler Planetarium and the Museum Campus, but because it's down a few steps with a seawall behind it, you can't see the museums or hear any car or foot traffic when you're lying on the sand. Relatively small compared to other city beaches, the beach here feels like a cove, with the land curving gently around it at both ends. The beach is clean and, amazingly, so are the bathrooms. If you're hungry, you can buy pizza, hotdogs, smoothies, ice cream, and other snacks for three bucks or less at the Windy City Café. The one downside is parking—if you don't get here early enough to score a meter, you'll have to pay $12 for the lot. Alternatively, the #12/Roosevelt and the #146 Inner Drive/Michigan Express buses make stops near the beach.

12th Street Beach is known as a good launching spot for kayakers, so you may see some paddlers in the water as well as sailboats farther offshore. Walk down to the south end of the beach, and you'll find even fewer people and a broader view of the city. The juxtaposition of water and skyscrapers is a reminder of what makes our city so beautiful and unique—the wide-open blue-green vista of the lake to the east and the towering urban skyline to the west. We may live in a big city in the heart of the Midwest, but fortunately, we're not landlocked.

✿ warner park and gardens

chicago's 50 best places to find peace and quiet

ADDRESS: 1446 W. Warner Avenue

Chicago, IL 60613

ADMISSION: Free

Tucked between two Victorian homes on a quiet North Side street, Warner Park looks like someone's side yard—albeit an extremely gorgeous one. Curving flowerbeds at the front screen much of the garden from view and beckon you to wander in and explore. Once you do, you'll find a delightful park that's much bigger than it appears at first glance.

For many years, Warner was the only privately owned public park in Chicago. In 1985, a nearby resident, Lois Buenger, took out a second mortgage to purchase and preserve the undeveloped property. With the help of neighborhood volunteers, Lois turned a nondescript city lot into an urban sanctuary spilling over with native plants and guarded by a magnificent gingko tree, all grown organically, without chemical pesticides or fertilizers. In 2001, Lois sold the land to NeighborSpace, a local nonprofit organization that buys small parcels of land all over the city, then works with local groups and businesses to maintain the spaces for public use.

The centerpiece of Warner Park is a wooden gazebo with built-in benches and a ceiling fan. It even has live electric outlets, so if you need a break from the usual work routine, you can tote your laptop to the park and work undisturbed among the greenery. The gazebo is up a few steps, providing a nice view of the whole space. The park has a rustic, homey feel to it, with its informal flowerbeds, trellis-style fence, winding brick sidewalk, vine-covered shed, and tables and chairs just begging for a picnic or friendly open-air card game. It's no wonder many couples have chosen to rent the park for their weddings.

When Lois Buenger sold Warner Park and Gardens to NeighborSpace, local politician Gene Schulter called her a hero for preserving the land for the community. Lois passed away in 2003, and I like to imagine there was a very special, very green spot saved for her in heaven. One thing's for sure, Chicago could use more heroes like Lois.

index by neighborhood

Northwest Side

North Side

Downtown

West Side

South Side

Northern Suburbs

Western Suburbs

Southern Suburbs

other city & company titles available from universe publishing

Chicago's 50 Best Places to Take Children
By Clare La Plante $14.95 • 0-7893-1078-3

City Baby 3rd Edition
By Pamela Weinberg and Kelly Ashton $18.95 • 0-7893-1348-0

City Baby Brooklyn
By Alison Lowenstein $18.95 • 0-7893-1344-8

City Baby Chicago
By Karin Horgan Sullivan $18.95 • 0-7893-1077-5

City Baby L.A. 2nd Edition
Linda Friedman Meadow and Lisa Rocchio $18.95 • 07893-1347-2

City Wedding 2nd Edition
By Joan Hamburg $18.95 • 0-7893-0856-8

The Cool Parents' Guide to All of New York 3rd Edition
By Alfred Gingold and Helen Rogan $14.95 • 0-7893-0857-6

Heavenly Weekends
By Susan Clemett and Gena Vandestienne $14.95 • 0-7893-0858-4

Literary Landmarks
By Bill Morgan, with photographs from the Museum of the
City of New York $16.95 • 0-7893-0854-1

The New York Book of Golf
By Nick Nicholas $14.95 • 0-7893-1055-4

The New York Book of Tea 3rd Edition
By Bo Niles $14.95 • 0-7893-0861-4

The New York Book of Wine
By Matthew DeBord $14.95 • 0-7893-0997-1

New York's 50+ Best Little Shops
By Ranjani Gopalarathinam $14.95 • 0-7893-1311-1

New York's 50 Best Places to Enjoy Breakfast and Brunch
By Courtney Baron $14.95 • 0-7893-1355-3

New York's 50+ Best Places to Enjoy Central Park and Other Green Retreats
By Karen Putnam $14.95 • 0-7893-1076-7

New York's 50 Best Places to Enjoy Dessert
By Andrea DiNoto and Paul Stiga $14.95 • 0-7893-0999-8

New York's 50 Best Places to Find Peace and Quiet 3rd Edition
By Allan Ishac $14.95 • 0-7893-0834-7

New York's 50 Best Places to Take Children 3rd Edition
By Allan Ishac $14.95 • 0-7893-1359-6

New York's 50 Best Places to Renew Body, Mind, and Spirit
By Beth Donnelly Cabán and Andrea Martin, with Allan Ishac
$14.95 • 0-7893-0835-5

New York's 100 Best Little Hotels 3rd Edition
By Allen Sperry $14.95 • 0-7893-0859-2

About the Author

Karin Horgan Sullivan fell so in love with Chicago
that she moved there without a job in 1987;
she's been there ever since. A freelance writer and
author of several books, she currently lives in
Oak Park with her husband and daughter.